WOMEN IN LEADERSHIP

ONE MINUTE BIBLE

For Mary —
A woman in all kinds of
leadership roles... Love, Candi

WOMEN IN LEADERSHIP

ONE MINUTE BIBLE

Daily Devotions to Guide
Today's Leading Women

BOB BRINER
with LAWRENCE KIMBROUGH

HOLMAN
REFERENCE

Nashville, Tennessee

One Minute Bible–*Women in Leadership*
Copyright © 1999 Broadman & Holman Publishers
Nashville, Tennessee, 37234
All rights reserved

0-8054-9193-7
Dewey Decimal Classification: 242.2
Subject Heading: CHRISTIAN WOMEN

Production Staff
Executive Editor: David Shepherd
Editor: Lawrence Kimbrough
Project Editor: Lloyd Mullens
Design Team: Wendell Overstreet, Anderson Thomas Graphics
Typesetting: TF Designs
Production: Kevin Kunce

Library of Congress Cataloging-in-Publication Data

Briner. Bob.
     One minute Bible : women in leadership / Bob Briner ; with Lawrence
Kimbrough.
        p. cm.
     Includes bibliographical references.
     ISBN 0-8054-9193-7
     1. Christian women Prayer-books and devotions–English. 2. Devotional
calendars. I. Kimbrough, Lawrence, 1963- . II. Title.
BV4844.B75   1999
242'.2–dc21
                                      99-15731
                                          CIP

Printed in United States of America
4 5 6 04
[Q]

CONTENTS

IT ALL STARTS HERE

The call to Christian leadership is a serious one. Leadership makes things happen. Leadership makes all the difference.

THE WORD FOR THE DAY

CHRISTIAN LEADERS FULLY UNDERSTAND THAT THEIR POSITION IS A GIFT FROM GOD, THAT THEIR INFLUENCE IS DEPENDENT ON HIS HELP.

—— ✇ ——

DON'T BE SURPRISED WHEN OTHERS WHINE, COMPLAIN, AND SECOND GUESS. LEADERS ARE PROVEN BY THEIR RESPONSES TO CHEAP SHOTS AND CHALLENGES.

—— ✇ ——

GOOD BOOKS AND TAPES ABOUND ON THE QUALITIES OF LEADERSHIP. BUT THE BEST ONE IS THE BOOK THAT HAS GOD'S WORD ON IT.

—— ✇ ——

MAKE SURE YOU'RE WILLING TO DO WHAT YOU ASK OF OTHERS.

Exodus 14:10–14, 21–22

As Pharaoh approached, the Israelites looked up, and there were the Egyptians, marching after them. They were terrified and cried out to the LORD.

They said to Moses, "Was it because there were no graves in Egypt that you brought us to the desert to die? What have you done to us by bringing us out of Egypt? Didn't we say to you in Egypt, 'Leave us alone; let us serve the Egyptians'? It would have been better for us to serve the Egyptians than to die in the desert!"

Moses answered the people, "Do not be afraid. Stand firm and you will see the deliverance the LORD will bring you today. The Egyptians you see today you will never see again. The LORD will fight for you; you need only to be still...."

Then Moses stretched out his hand over the sea, and all that night the LORD drove the sea back with a strong east wind and turned it into dry land. The waters were divided, and the Israelites went through the sea on dry ground, with a wall of water on their right and on their left.

THE VOICE OF WISDOM

What is taking the place of traditional management today? Traditional managers are being replaced by people who have a different approach to getting things done. Management is being replaced by leadership.

Leadership Principle

NUMBER 1

EVERYTHING RISES AND FALLS ON LEADERSHIP.

Leaders are able to influence others even when they have no formal authority. Leaders are able to visualize clearly what needs to be accomplished. They are able to organize others to believe in and support this vision, mobilize the resources to get action, and build relationships for continued progress. Wherever they are, leaders do not rely on a base of formal authority or a position of power. Their effectiveness comes from their abilities to develop followers–contributors to the shared goals of the group.

Management entails getting things done through others. Leadership is more aptly defined as getting this done *with* others. If leadership equals influence, all Christian women have the opportunity to influence others. In the roles of wives, mothers, daughters, and friends, we influence through our words and our lives.

–SUSAN HUNT

Let the daunting size of your task and the sheer weight of your responsibility keep you daily at the feet of God.

SEEKING GOD'S FACE

God's will is much bigger than churches and Christian companies.
Wherever you lead, you need Him leading you.

THE WEARING OF SACKCLOTH WAS A SIGN OF REPENTANCE AND CONFESSION. WANT TO ENTERTAIN GOD'S WILL? MAKE SURE YOUR OWN HOUSE IS CLEAN.

APPROACHING THE PERSIAN KING UNINVITED WAS A DEATH SENTENCE. DOING WHAT GOD SAYS CAN SOMETIMES BE VERY COSTLY.

WHO KNOWS BUT THAT YOU'VE BEEN PUT IN YOUR PLACE OF LEADERSHIP "FOR SUCH A TIME AS THIS"?

FASTING, IN ALL ITS UNLEGAL-ISTIC FORMS, IS STILL A VERY VALID WAY OF HEARING FROM GOD.

Esther 4:4-5, 13-16

When Esther's maids and eunuchs came and told her about Mordecai, she was in great distress. She sent clothes for him to put on instead of his sackcloth, but he would not accept them.

Then Esther summoned Hathach, one of the king's eunuchs assigned to attend her, and ordered him to find out what was troubling Mordecai and why....

He sent back this answer: "Do not think that because you are in the king's house you alone of all the Jews will escape. For if you remain silent at this time, relief and deliverance for the Jews will arise from another place, but you and your father's family will perish. And who knows but that you have come to royal position for such a time as this?"

Then Esther sent this reply to Mordecai: "Go, gather together all the Jews who are in Susa, and fast for me. Do not eat or drink for three days, night or day. I and my maids will fast as you do. When this is done, I will go to the king, even though it is against the law. And if I perish, I perish."

THE VOICE OF WISDOM

If we are really serious in our search for God's will, we can be assured that we shall know it. Once we know His will, we have no option but–by faith and in His strength–to obey it, because the Scriptures tell us that when we know what to do and don't do it, is sin.

Yes, it is a bit frightening, a bit risky. When we take our willing hearts and say, "Lord, I totally trust You. I deny myself and am totally available to You," and really mean it, God will take us at our word.

He might even put us to the test, to see how sincere we really are. Until action is required, words and faith are easy. It may mean adjustments, large and small. It may tax our emotions and our nerves. But whatever it is, we can be assured of one thing: It will be worth it, and He will give us the strength to do it. "As for God, his way is perfect" (2 Samuel 22:31).

The only safe place is in the center of God's will. It is not only the safest place. It is also the most rewarding and the most satisfying place to be. As Mother Teresa said, "Holiness is doing God's will with a smile."

–GIGI GRAHAM TCHIVIDJIAN

The breakthrough moment in finding the will of God is realizing that you need Him even more than His answer.

TIME FOR ACTION

You've made your plans, thought everything through.
Now it's time to put it into practice. Are you ready?

THE WORD FOR THE DAY

THIS IS A RATHER GRUESOME EXAMPLE—(SORRY)—BUT WHEN FACED WITH THE CHALLENGES OF THE DAY, LEADERS MUST RESPOND.

❧

YOU CAN SPOT THE EMERGING LEADERS IN YOUR GROUP OR ORGANIZATION BY SEEING WHO TAKES CHARGE WHEN OTHERS TAKE COVER.

❧

DECISIVE ACTION ALWAYS REQUIRES AN ELEMENT OF BRAVERY.

❧

YOU DON'T HAVE TO BE ON THE FRONTLINES TO MAKE SIZABLE CONTRIBUTIONS TOWARD YOUR TEAM'S SUCCESS.

Judges 4:15a, 17-21, 23

At Barak's advance, the LORD routed Sisera and all his chariots and army by the sword....

Sisera, however, fled on foot to the tent of Jael, the wife of Heber the Kenite, because there were friendly relations between Jabin king of Hazor and the clan of Heber the Kenite.

Jael went out to meet Sisera and said to him, "Come, my lord, come right in. Don't be afraid." So he entered her tent, and she put a covering over him.

"I'm thirsty," he said. "Please give me some water." She opened a skin of milk, gave him a drink, and covered him up.

"Stand in the doorway of the tent," he told her. "If someone comes by and asks you, 'Is anyone here?' say 'No.'"

But Jael, Heber's wife, picked up a tent peg and a hammer and went quietly to him while he lay fast asleep, exhausted. She drove the peg through his temple into the ground, and he died....

On that day God subdued Jabin, the Canaanite king, before the Israelites.

THE VOICE OF WISDOM

For the last twelve hours I have known something so dreadful that I can't even imagine it. I have the feeling that I'd like to go to bed and pull the covers over my head and stay there for six weeks, and then peek out and see if it is all over. If it isn't, I'd like to crawl under again.

The day had a dream-like quality. George told me last night that it [the Persian Gulf War] would start tonight. God knows they have given Saddam every chance.

All America is praying and we are, too. George told me last night that it is always on his mind. As we said our prayers and as he read the message he is going to give the American people tonight, his voice cracked and his eyes got misty. I asked him over coffee in bed this morning as he read through tonight's message who wrote the speech, and he said that he had. I had wondered how it could have remained a secret if it had been written by the speech writers. George told me that he might come home and have lunch with me and take a nap. I guess that sleep did not come too well last night.

–BARBARA BUSH

Make your next important decision be the one to seek God's wisdom on your next important decision.

SHARE THE VISION

It may come as second nature to you, but people can't see the big picture the way you do. Paint it with a passion.

THE WORD FOR THE DAY

GIDEON HAD HIS DOUBTS. BUT WHEN THE TIME CAME FOR LEADING THE CHARGE, HE THREW HIS FULL WEIGHT BEHIND THE MISSION.

———— ❧ ————

GOD HAD TRIMMED GIDEON'S ARMY DOWN TO FIGHTING SIZE. SOMETIMES THE VISION CAN ONLY BE REACHED WITH THE RIGHT PEOPLE.

———— ❧ ————

BEFORE YOU CAN REVEAL YOUR VISION, YOU MUST FIRST HAVE IT CLEAR IN YOUR MIND. CAN YOU PUT YOUR PLAN INTO WORDS?

———— ❧ ————

EVEN IN NON-CHRISTIAN ENVIRONMENTS, THIS IS A GOOD TIME TO REVEAL YOUR DEPENDENCE ON GOD.

Judges 7:17-22a

"Watch me," he told them. "Follow my lead. When I get to the edge of the camp, do exactly as I do. When I and all who are with me blow our trumpets, then from all around the camp blow yours and shout, 'For the LORD and for Gideon.'"

Gideon and the hundred men with him reached the edge of the camp at the beginning of the middle watch, just after they had changed the guard. They blew their trumpets and broke the jars that were in their hands.

The three companies blew the trumpets and smashed the jars. Grasping the torches in their left hands and holding in their right hands the trumpets they were to blow, they shouted, "A sword for the LORD and for Gideon!"

While each man held his position around the camp, all the Midianites ran, crying out as they fled.

When the three hundred trumpets sounded, the LORD caused the men throughout the camp to turn on each other with their swords.

THE VOICE OF WISDOM

Leadership & Principle

NUMBER 4

LEADERS NURTURE A VISION AND AT THE RIGHT TIME DECLARE IT, SO OTHERS CAN RALLY TO THE CAUSE.

Knowing that the Holy Spirit will strengthen your leadership underlines your need for the cooperative effort of others. Who can be a visionary leader without followers? Those you lead should:

1. *Agree with your goals and objectives.* You must have acquainted them not only with the projected outcome, but also the many tasks leading to it. With your encouragement, they should consider their assigned role important to the accomplishment of the goals.

2. *Be able to handle the responsibility assigned.* If you have seriously considered the qualities and abilities of those you lead, you will be careful to assign tasks that each can accomplish with satisfaction.

3. *Help your coworkers develop a spirit of faithfulness, to be individuals you can count on to complete their work on time and satisfactorily.* Christian leaders can look to Jesus for guidance in this. Jesus said, "Whoever can be trusted with very little can also be trusted with much" (Luke 16:10). This infers that by beginning with small jobs and trusting your helpers to perform them well, you can then give them greater responsibilities.

–GLADYS ISRAELS & T. R. HOLLINGSWORTH

Give your latest dream some time to grow and develop. And ask God for the right time to bring it into the open.

A MATTER OF TIME

You know how busy you get. But are you using your time effectively? Or does it feel more like time is using you?

THE WORD FOR THE DAY

"COUNTING THE COST" IS A BIBLICAL IDEA THAT APPLIES TO EVERY AREA OF THE LEADER'S LIFE.

———— ❧ ————

JESUS OFTEN USED SIMPLE WORD PICTURES TO CONVEY IMPORTANT CONCEPTS. TRY USING THIS APPROACH IN YOUR OWN COMMUNICATION.

———— ❧ ————

JESUS DEMANDED TOTAL ALLEGIANCE FROM HIS FOLLOWERS. FROM THE LOOK OF YOUR DAILY SCHEDULE, DOES HE HAVE YOURS?

———— ❧ ————

"HE WHO HAS EARS TO HEAR, LET HIM HEAR." DON'T ASSUME THOSE WHO HEAR YOU ALWAYS UNDERSTAND EXACTLY WHAT YOU'RE SAYING.

Luke 14:28-35

"Suppose one of you wants to build a tower. Will he not first sit down and estimate the cost to see if he has enough money to complete it?

"For if he lays the foundation and is not able to finish it, everyone who sees it will ridicule him, saying, 'This fellow began to build and was not able to finish.'

"Or suppose a king is about to go to war against another king. Will he not first sit down and consider whether he is able with ten thousand men to oppose the one coming against him with twenty thousand?

"If he is not able, he will send a delegation while the other is still a long way off and will ask for terms of peace.

"In the same way, any of you who does not give up everything he has cannot be my disciple.

"Salt is good, but if it loses its saltiness, how can it be made salty again?

"It is fit neither for the soil nor for the manure pile; it is thrown out.

"He who has ears to hear, let him hear."

THE VOICE OF WISDOM

I tend to assume that if I'm really busy, I must be doing something productive.

But if the devil can keep us busy doing things that are insignificant and without eternal value, he can keep us from our divine appointments and from hearing God's Word clearly when God is speaking to us. He can steal our joy. There is nothing worse than not knowing where we're going, and killing ourselves to get there.

Some days my husband will ask, "What did you do today?"

"I was so busy!" I'll reply enthusiastically. Then he'll say, "Well, what'd you do?" I have no idea. But I was so busy doing it!

It reminds me of the advice the Cheshire cat gave to Alice in Wonderland when she asked him which path to take at an intersection.

"Where are you going?" the cat asked.

"I have no idea," Alice replied.

"When you don't know where you're going, any road will do," he answered.

I've finally realized that if something has no significant value, it doesn't deserve my time. Life is not a dress rehearsal, and I'll never get this day again.

—SHERI ROSE SHEPHERD

Leadership Principle

NUMBER 5

LEADERSHIP IS AN EXPENSIVE CALLING. IT WILL COST YOU TIME THAT WOULD BE EASIER TO WASTE.

_____
_____
_____
_____
_____
_____
_____
_____
_____
_____
_____
_____
_____
_____
_____
_____
_____
_____
_____

As you examine your schedule and make your plans, be sure your activities are lining up with your true priorities.

YOUR WORD ON IT

If you had it to do over again, you would never have promised to do what you said. But you did. So go do it.

BE CAREFUL WHAT YOU PROMISE, BECAUSE TRUE LEADERS EXPECT TO LIVE UP TO THEIR WORDS.

———— ❧ ————

SADLY, PEOPLE ARE NOT ALWAYS WHAT THEY APPEAR TO BE. EXERCISE CAUTION AND DISCERNMENT IN DEALING WITH THOSE YOU DON'T KNOW.

———— ❧ ————

"THE MEN OF ISRAEL DID NOT INQUIRE OF THE LORD." AND THAT'S WHERE THEY MADE THEIR FIRST MISTAKE.

———— ❧ ————

BACKING OUT OF A PROMISE ONLY MAKES THE PROBLEM WORSE—AND MAY CREATE EVEN MORE HARDSHIPS AND HARD FEELINGS DOWN THE ROAD.

Joshua 9:3-6, 14-16, 18a

When the people of Gibeon heard what Joshua had done to Jericho and Ai, they resorted to a ruse: They went as a delegation whose donkeys were loaded with worn-out sacks and old wineskins, cracked and mended. The men put worn and patched sandals on their feet and wore old clothes. All the bread of their food supply was dry and moldy.

Then they went to Joshua in the camp at Gilgal and said to him and the men of Israel, "We have come from a distant country; make a treaty with us. . . ."

The men of Israel sampled their provisions but did not inquire of the LORD.

Then Joshua made a treaty of peace with them to let them live, and the leaders of the assembly ratified it by oath.

Three days after they made the treaty with the Gibeonites, the Israelites heard that they were neighbors, living near them. . . .

But the Israelites did not attack them, because the leaders of the assembly had sworn an oath to them by the LORD.

THE VOICE OF WISDOM

Leadership Principle

NUMBER 6

LEADERS HONOR THEIR PROMISES, EVEN WHEN THEY HAVE BEEN WRONG IN MAKING THEM.

Now and then we hear of people whose word is as good as their bond, but far too often we find that "word of honor" is used carefully, then forgotten or ignored.

One's word is of infinitely more worth than money. If money is lost, more money, and just as good, is to be had; but if you pledge your word and do not redeem it, you have lost something that cannot be replaced. It is intangible perhaps, but nevertheless valuable to you.

A person who cannot be depended upon by others, in time, becomes unable to depend upon himself. It seems in some subtle way to undermine and weaken the character when we do not hold ourselves strictly responsible for what we say.

And what a tangle it makes of all our undertakings when people do not keep their promises. How much pleasanter it would be, and how much more would be accomplished, if we did not give our word unless we intended to keep it, so that we would all know what we could depend upon.

If everybody did his duty well in the smaller things, there would be no failures when the greater duties presented themselves.

–LAURA INGALLS WILDER

Have you committed to something, to someone? Promise God you'll learn from it. But first, follow through on it.

KEEP ON KEEPING ON

Some days you don't feel like getting out of bed. Or seeing anybody.
That's when you learn where your strength lies.

THE WORD FOR THE DAY

"THE LORD IS NEAR."
ALWAYS TRY TO KEEP YOUR
DAILY DEMANDS IN ETERNAL
PERSPECTIVE. WHEN UNDER
PRESSURE OR OVERWHELMED,
MAKE PRAYER YOUR FIRST LINE
OF DEFENSE.

⸙

THINK OF GOD'S PEACE AS A
"GUARD," PROTECTING YOUR
MIND FROM SURRENDER AND
DISCOURAGEMENT.

⸙

HARD TIMES, LEAN TIMES,
CHALLENGING TIMES—THAT IS
WHERE TRUE LEADERS ARE
MADE.

⸙

YOU CAN DO ALL THINGS
THROUGH CHRIST. ARE YOU
LEADING AS THOUGH YOU
BELIEVE IT?

Philippians 4:4-8, 11b-13

Rejoice in the Lord always. I will say it again: Rejoice! Let your gentleness be evident to all. The Lord is near.

Do not be anxious about anything, but in everything, by prayer and petition, with thanksgiving, present your requests to God.

And the peace of God, which transcends all understanding, will guard your hearts and your minds in Christ Jesus.

Finally, brothers, whatever is true, whatever is noble, whatever is right, whatever is pure, whatever is lovely, whatever is admirable–if anything is excellent or praiseworthy–think about such things. . . .

I have learned to be content whatever the circumstances. I know what it is to be in need, and I know what it is to have plenty. I have learned the secret of being content in any and every situation, whether well fed or hungry, whether living in plenty or in want.

I can do everything through him who gives me strength.

THE VOICE OF WISDOM

Paul talked about "press[ing] on" toward the goal. "I pictured myself inside a car, chugging along the highways of life. When I came to a hill, I would put on the gas ("press on," so to speak.) When I came to a slope, I would tend to coast down. But then I would find myself unprepared for the next hill. Did the apostle Paul mean to "press on" continually? I concluded he did.

Suddenly, I mentally transformed my car's fuel into joy, and noticed the tank registered full. But unless I stepped on the accelerator, nothing would happen. No joy would flow. When I did press down, joy would be released–enough, I noticed, to maneuver me successfully through any road condition I faced. The responsibility clearly lay with me.

Christ's determination to endure the pain of the cross was what released the joy that was "set before Him." Because the apostle Paul "pressed on," he eventually learned to be content in any situation. If I could just hang in there, being faithful to my own tasks, God would make me joyful and content. The responsibility is mine, but the power is His.

–PEG RANKIN

Leadership Principle

NUMBER 7

LEADERS REMAIN MOTIVATED IN SPITE OF CIRCUMSTANCES, NOT BECAUSE OF THEM.

Next time you're having one of those days, be sure the only reason you're lowering your head is to barge ahead.

DOWNRIGHT UPRIGHT

Not too many people remember the days of black and white. But people who lead with integrity still see things that way.

THE WORD FOR THE DAY

NOTICE THAT GOD WAS THE ONE POINTING JOB OUT TO SATAN. HE IS APPARENTLY WILLING TO LET THE DEVIL TAKE HIS BEST CRACKS AT GOD'S MOST FAITHFUL FOLKS.

———

DON'T BE SURPRISED WHEN YOUR INTEGRITY IS CHALLENGED. YOU CAN'T KNOW HOW STRONG IT IS UNTIL IT'S TESTED.

———

THERE WILL ALWAYS BE PEOPLE LIKE JOB'S WIFE HANDING OUT EASY-WAY ADVICE. BE CAREFUL WHOSE COUNSEL YOU TAKE STOCK IN.

———

"JOB DID NOT SIN IN WHAT HE SAID." WORDS CAN BE A KEY INTEGRITY INDICATOR.

Job 2:3-5, 7-10

Then the LORD said to Satan, "Have you considered my servant Job? There is no one on earth like him; he is blameless and upright, a man who fears God and shuns evil. And he still maintains his integrity, though you incited me against him to ruin him without any reason."

"Skin for skin!" Satan replied. "A man will give all he has for his own life. But stretch out your hand and strike his flesh and bones, and he will surely curse you to your face...."

So Satan went out from the presence of the LORD and afflicted Job with painful sores from the soles of his feet to the top of his head. Then Job took a piece of broken pottery and scraped himself with it as he sat among the ashes.

His wife said to him, "Are you still holding on to your integrity? Curse God and die!"

He replied, "You are talking like a foolish woman. Shall we accept good from God, and not trouble?" In all this, Job did not sin in what he said.

THE VOICE OF WISDOM

One evening my class was rehearsing a play in the school cafeteria. When I was busy with the cast on stage, a few students took some ice cream bars from the school kitchen. After consideration, the principal instructed me to give them an F in conduct for that grading period.

The four students were all members of the school's honor society and leaders among the student body. The other members of the honor society voted to drop them from membership.

The chairman of the board visited the principal and told her that, because of the political influence of one family involved, he might not be able to save her job unless she changed her ruling. The principal said, "Unless you can show me that those boys did right, I cannot alter my decision."

Education was a career of great importance to that lady, yet she laid it on the line because she would not bend her standards under pressure. She did not lose her job, but she was willing to sacrifice it if necessary.

Truth does not change with circumstances—neither do leaders who have integrity.

–GEORGIA SETTLE

Leadership Principle

NUMBER 8

STRONG LEADERS MUST BE WILLING TO STAND ALONE WITH THEIR CONVICTIONS.

If you want to be known as a woman of integrity, what are some things you can do today to earn that reputation?

YOU'LL DO JUST FINE

Even confident women can feel inferior sometimes. Don't make yourself feel worse by trying to be somebody else.

THE WORD FOR THE DAY

TRYING TO "COMMEND OUR-
SELVES" THROUGH ANYTHING
OTHER THAN OUR WORK AND
LIFE IS A WASTE
OF TIME AND ENERGY.

WHY SHOULD YOU FEEL LESS
CONFIDENT IN YOUR ABILITIES
JUST BECAUSE YOU DON'T LOOK
YOUR BEST THAT DAY?

"WHERE THE SPIRIT OF THE
LORD IS, THERE IS
FREEDOM". . . TO BE YOUR-
SELF, TO BE WHO GOD MADE
YOU TO BE.

NOT HIDING BEHIND PRETEN-
SIONS CAN BREAK THE PLASTIC
MASK OF THE WHOLE ROOM,
AND MAKE EVERYONE
MORE AT EASE.

2 Corinthians 3:1-6a, 17-18

Are we beginning to commend ourselves again? Or do we need, like some people, letters of recommendation to you or from you?

You yourselves are our letter, written on our hearts, known and read by everybody. You show that you are a letter from Christ, the result of our ministry, written not with ink but with the Spirit of the living God, not on tablets of stone but on tablets of human hearts.

Such confidence as this is ours through Christ before God. Not that we are competent in ourselves to claim anything for ourselves, but our competence comes from God.

He has made us competent as ministers of a new covenant—not of the letter but of the Spirit. . . .

Now the Lord is the Spirit, and where the Spirit of the Lord is, there is freedom.

And we, who with unveiled faces all reflect the Lord's glory, are being transformed into his likeness with ever-increasing glory, which comes from the Lord, who is the Spirit.

THE VOICE OF WISDOM

How did your conference go? I prayed for you all weekend while I was doing mine in St. Louis. I had quite an experience getting there. At the airport, going up the stone steps to my gate, I tripped and heard the awful sound made as my two front teeth chipped off against the next step up.

Of course, I split my lip. Oh, I was a real doll all weekend! Strangely enough, though, I think it was the most blessed weekend of ministry in my life.

Now the dentist has remade my teeth and my lip is healing, but what I will remember from it is that God hates pride. He certainly dealt with mine in a dramatic way.

Blessings on you . . .

I cringed inwardly when I read about her accident, asking myself, *Would I have continued through the weekend as graciously as she did?* Yet God asked her to press on even when her appearance suddenly slipped to what the world considers "below par." God doesn't use us based on what we look like. He uses us based on the condition of our souls.

–JUDITH COUCHMAN

Leadership & Principle

NUMBER 9

BE COMFORTABLE BEING YOURSELF IN ANY SITUATION.

Next time the nervous tension of feeling unqualified gets the best of you, just try to be the best you you can be.

THE BIG ONES

Decisions and demands can get very fatiguing, but not to those who filte
them through a set system of core values.

THE WORD FOR THE DAY

THE TEN COMMANDMENTS ARE
OVER 3,500 YEARS OLD. AND
STILL RIGHT ON THE MARK.

―――― ⟡ ――――

YOU WOULD EXPECT THE WIS-
DOM OF THE AGES TO BE LONG,
COMPLEX, HARD-TO-GRASP.
THESE LAWS ARE SHORT, SUC-
CINCT, STRONG. YOURS
SHOULD BE, TOO.

―――― ⟡ ――――

GOD COMES FIRST. HIS WILL
MUST BE YOUR PRIORITY IN
ANYTHING YOU UNDERTAKE IN
LIFE, BUSINESS, OR MINISTRY
IF YOU WANT IT TO GENUINELY
SUCCEED.

―――― ⟡ ――――

THESE PRINCIPLES ARE NOT
TRUE BECAUSE THEY WORK.
THEY WORK BECAUSE
THEY ARE TRUE.

Exodus 20:3-4, 7-8, 12-1?

"You shall have no other gods before me.

"You shall not make for yourself an idol in th
form of anything in heaven above or on the eart.
beneath or in the waters below....

"You shall not misuse the name of the LOR.
your God, for the LORD will not hold anyone guil.
less who misuses his name.

"Remember the Sabbath day by keeping it holy...

"Honor your father and your mother, so tha
you may live long in the land the LORD your Go
is giving you.

"You shall not murder.

"You shall not commit adultery.

"You shall not steal.

"You shall not give false testimony against you
neighbor.

"You shall not covet your neighbor's house. Yo
shall not covet your neighbor's wife, or h
manservant or maidservant, his ox or donkey, c
anything that belongs to your neighbor."

THE VOICE OF WISDOM

Personal choices encompass every aspect of life. When these reflect the secure absolutes of truth found in God's Word, stability is ensured. Even the wise sayings of respected persons or the practical insights of leaders can neither supply the foundation nor substitute for the security that only God's Word can provide.

Augustine, an early historian of the church, stated, "The morality of an act depends neither on its consequences nor its essential nature nor its motivation but solely on whether it is in accordance with the will of God."

We need to evaluate our thoughts, considerations, and decisions against the truth of God's Word, and we need to help those with whom we are in contact–both Christian and non-Christian–to begin to search God's Word and to "think biblically." We don't need to impose our thinking upon them or attempt to force them to agree with our conclusions of faith. Our role is simply to guide, leading them to the One who holds all truth. Truly he is "the way, the truth, and the life."

–LINDA MCGINN

Leadership & Principle

NUMBER 10

LEADERS MUST HAVE CORE VALUES, CLEARLY ARTICULATED, EASILY UNDERSTOOD, ON THE MAJOR ISSUES OF LIFE.

Do you have a written mission statement for your life? They are essential in helping you stay true to your values.

MOST EXCELLENT

You're on. No dry runs. No practice drills.
Today, you are in the spotlight at center stage. Give it all you've got.

THE FIRST STEP TOWARD EXCELLENCE IS TO BE GRATEFUL FOR THE GIFTS AND OPPORTUNITIES GOD HAS GIVEN.

THE SECOND STEP IS HUMILITY. "WHO THEN AM I" SOLOMON SAID, "TO BUILD A TEMPLE FOR HIM?" REMEMBER WHO'S REALLY IN CHARGE OF THIS THING.

EXCELLENCE DOESN'T MEAN BEING BETTER THAN EVERYONE ELSE, JUST BEING YOUR BEST.

THE POWERFUL AND INFLUENTIAL WILL NOTICE YOUR HIGH WORK ETHIC. BE SURE THEY KNOW WHO IT COMES FROM.

(SEE PROVERBS 22:29.)

2 Chronicles 2:3a, 5–9

Solomon sent this message to Hiram king of Tyre . . .

"The temple I am going to build will be great, because our God is greater than all other gods.

"But who is able to build a temple for him, since the heavens, even the highest heavens, cannot contain him? Who then am I to build a temple for him, except as a place to burn sacrifices before him?

"Send me, therefore, a man skilled to work in gold and silver, bronze and iron, and in purple, crimson and blue yarn, and experienced in the art of engraving, to work in Judah and Jerusalem with my skilled craftsmen, whom my father David provided.

"Send me also cedar, pine and algum logs from Lebanon, for I know that your men are skilled in cutting timber there. My men shall work with yours to provide me with plenty of timber, because the temple I build must be large and magnificent."

THE VOICE OF WISDOM

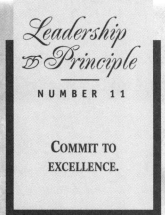

Leadership & Principle

NUMBER 11

COMMIT TO EXCELLENCE.

If there has ever been a time when we need great leaders with commitment to great ideas, it is now. We need them in your town and mine. We need them in business, in government, and in community groups.

I can hear someone saying that being great is a tall order. Don't be put off by the word *great*. People need examples of greatness to show them the power of commitment.

Most people go through life saying, "Well, that's good enough." Good enough for whom, for what? For the difficult and challenging times we live in? For a future that needs deeply committed leaders?

Winston Churchill said, "We make a living by what we get, but we make a life by what we give." There are people and projects in this world that are worth the struggle for greatness.

But greatness is not the goal. It is the pursuit of greatness that will set you apart from people who are willing to settle for good enough. It's your commitment to giving that will make you a leader who can make a difference. Good is the enemy of great.

–SHEILA MURRAY BETHEL

You may not feel like you have the time to do everything well. But doing everything well is what time is for.

UP WITH PEOPLE

Some people are easy to like. Others . . . well, not so easy. But everyone you meet deserves to know that you care.

THE WORD FOR THE DAY

JESUS TOOK TIME TO GET AWAY, BUT HE RECOGNIZED WHEN PEOPLE NEEDED HIM MORE THAN HE NEEDED REST.

THE DISCIPLES FELT THEY HAD FIRST DIBS ON JESUS. BUT HE WAS WILLING TO OFFEND HIS INNER CIRCLE IN ORDER TO BE KIND AND INCLUSIVE TO THOSE ON THE FRINGES.

IF YOU EVER REACH THE POINT WHERE PEOPLE ARE IN YOUR WAY, YOUR LIFE HAS GOTTEN OUT OF PROPORTION.

IT DOESN'T TAKE A LOT OF TIME TO SHOW PEOPLE YOU CARE ABOUT THEM. THEY'LL SEE IT IN YOUR EYES IF IT'S TRUE.

Mark 6:30-37a

The apostles gathered around Jesus and reported to him all they had done and taught. Then because so many people were coming and going that they did not even have a chance to eat, he said to them, "Come with me by yourselves to a quiet place and get some rest."

So they went away by themselves in a boat to a solitary place. But many who saw them leaving recognized them and ran on foot from all the towns and got there ahead of them.

When Jesus landed and saw a large crowd, he had compassion on them, because they were like sheep without a shepherd. So he began teaching them many things.

By this time it was late in the day, so his disciples came to him. "This is a remote place," they said, "and it's already very late. Send the people away so that they can go to the surrounding countryside and villages and buy themselves something to eat."

But he answered, "You give them something to eat."

THE VOICE OF WISDOM

It's one thing to know we should love people we don't like. It's another thing to make it happen. A prerequisite to developing love actions toward those unlikable people in your life is to change your thinking. There's no way you can keep on thinking of how irritating they are or how thoughtless or annoying, and then turn around and have love actions toward them. What you think will come out in your actions.

So remember God's love for you. Change your thinking about these unlikable people in your life, and then pray for them. Sincerely, regularly, pray for their welfare. As much as you know about them, pray in detail for them. Ask God to show you what love actions to take toward them. Jesus taught us to pray for our enemies and those who despitefully use us. As you pray about those people you don't like, ask God for wisdom in knowing which love actions are appropriate for each person. Does one require a lot of patience? Does one require compassion or endurance? When you have discerned the need, set your will to act with those love actions toward those people.

–MARY WHELCHEL

Leadership Principle
NUMBER 12

GOOD LEADERS WORK HARD TO DEVELOP THEIR PEOPLE SKILLS.

You want to reach your goals and objectives. But connecting with the people you lead should be near the top of the list.

ACTIVE VOICE

You have a right to talk as brave and boldly as you want to, as long as you bear the responsibility for acting on it.

THE WORD FOR THE DAY

BEFORE ASKING THE PEOPLE TO GIVE, DAVID DUG DEEPLY INTO HIS OWN POCKETS TO SHOW THE WAY. WHEN YOU ASK BIG THINGS OF OTHERS, BE PREPARED TO DO BIG THINGS YOURSELF.

THE GIFTS CAME WILLINGLY FOLLOWING THE EXAMPLE SET BY DAVID. BOLD ACTION ON YOUR PART WILL BREED SPONTANEITY IN OTHERS.

YOUR DREAMS ARE ONLY AS GREAT AS THE PRICE YOU'RE WILLING TO PAY FOR THEM.

"GREATER LOVE HAS NO ONE THAN THIS, THAT HE LAY DOWN HIS LIFE FOR HIS FRIENDS" (JOHN 15:13).

1 Chronicles 29:1–3, 6

Then King David said to the whole assembly: "My son Solomon, the one whom God has chosen, is young and inexperienced. The task is great, because this palatial structure is not for man but for the LORD God.

"With all my resources I have provided for the temple of my God–gold for the gold work, silver for the silver, bronze for the bronze, iron for the iron and wood for the wood, as well as onyx for the settings, turquoise, stones of various colors, and all kinds of fine stone and marble–all of these in large quantities.

"Besides, in my devotion to the temple of my God I now give my personal treasures of gold and silver for the temple of my God, over and above everything I have provided for this holy temple . . ."

Then the leaders of families, the officers of the tribes of Israel, the commanders of thousands and commanders of hundreds, and the officials in charge of the king's work gave willingly.

THE VOICE OF WISDOM

The Reformation produced many heroes and heroines of faith. In the Netherlands, Charles V imposed severe penalties on anyone who possessed a Bible or Reformed writings, preached Reformed doctrines, harbored such preachers, or attended their meetings. Wendelmuta Klaus, a widow and known Protestant from North Holland, was apprehended in 1527. She was examined before the Stadholder of Holland, Count van Hoogst, and a great council.

When told that unless she renounced her errors a dreadful death awaited her, she replied: "If the power is given you from above, I am prepared to suffer."

Many more questions were put to her, all of which she answered readily with Scripture. Her examiners were enraged at her calmness and sent her back to prison.

She was brought the next day before the council, and after another short examination was condemned to death. From the council hall she was led out to a scaffold, strangled, and then burnt.

"I cannot be silent, dear sister, I cannot be silent." And the words of Wendelmuta Klaus continue to be heard.

–SUSAN HUNT

Leadership & Principle

NUMBER 13

BACK UP YOUR WORDS WITH BOLD ACTION, AND OTHERS WILL FOLLOW.

Think of some concrete ways you can demonstrate to your team just how seriously you take your shared mission.

WITHOUT A PRAYER?

We tend to think getting an answer from God is the main reason we pray. The main reason we pray is to be praying.

THE WORD FOR THE DAY

EVER FEEL LIKE YOU'RE BOTH-
ERING GOD WITH YOUR
REQUESTS? HE SAID HIMSELF
THAT WE SHOULD "PRAY AND
NOT GIVE UP."

———— ❧ ————

YOUR ADVERSARY MAY BE—A
DEADLINE, A BIG DECISION, A
THREAT TO YOUR LEADERSHIP,
ANYTHING. BUT YOUR APPEAL
SHOULD BE FOR GOD'S JUSTICE
TO PREVAIL.

———— ❧ ————

THE LORD'S BUSINESS HOURS
ARE 24/7, OPEN "DAY AND
NIGHT" TO HEAR THE CRIES OF
HIS CHILDREN.

———— ❧ ————

COULD IT BE THAT PERSISTENT
PRAYER BUILDS MORE FAITH
THAN AN IMMEDIATE ANSWER?

Luke 18:1-8

Then Jesus told his disciples a parable to show them that they should always pray and not give up.

He said: "In a certain town there was a judge who neither feared God nor cared about men.

"And there was a widow in that town who kept coming to him with the plea, 'Grant me justice against my adversary.'

"For some time he refused. But finally he said to himself, 'Even though I don't fear God or care about men, yet because this widow keeps bothering me, I will see that she gets justice, so that she won't eventually wear me out with her coming!'

And the Lord said, "Listen to what the unjust judge says. And will not God bring about justice for his chosen ones, who cry out to him day and night? Will he keep putting them off?

"I tell you, he will see that they get justice, and quickly. However, when the Son of Man comes, will he find faith on the earth?"

THE VOICE OF WISDOM

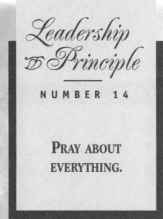

Leadership & Principle

NUMBER 14

PRAY ABOUT EVERYTHING.

How do you handle the issues you face each day as you confront life in the real world? Do you find yourself in God's Word, prayerfully seeking God's guidance and help? Or do you immediately turn to others to tell you what to do?

I don't know about you, but sometimes when a crises arises, I find myself asking others to pray before I've talked to God about the situation myself. I've come to realize that God wants me to read His Word and talk to Him first. Actually He wants me to talk to Him always.

We constantly carry on a personal conversation with ourselves. We evaluate every situation. We review conversations with others over and over in our minds. We carry on an internal discussion about life and our evaluation of it.

I believe God wants us to invite Him into that conversation. That's what I believe Paul means when he tells the Thessalonians to "Pray without ceasing" (1 Thess. 5:17). God never gives us a command that we can't fulfill. So instead of talking to yourself, why not start talking with God?

–LINDA MCGINN

God has more at stake in your prayer than a yes or no answer. Ask Him to do what He needs to do with you.

UNDER CONTROL

Leaders who can make themselves do the right things will come a lot closer to making other people do them, as well.

THE WORD FOR THE DAY

LEADERS SHOULD KNOW THEIR STRENGTHS, BUT ALSO THEIR OWN WEAKNESSES.

—∞—

IT'S EASY TO BECOME BLINDED TO YOUR OWN SUBTLE SINS, BUT STAYING ACCOUNTABLE TO A GROUP OF GOOD FRIENDS WILL HELP KEEP YOU HONEST.

—∞—

GOD WILL ALWAYS FORGIVE. BUT LACK OF CHARACTER WILL COST YOU YOUR SEAT OF INFLUENCE.

—∞—

THE BEST DEFENSE AGAINST SELF-DESTRUCTION IS TO KEEP YOUR HEAD IN THE PROMISES OF GOD. EVERY DAY. EVERY MOMENT.

1 Samuel 15:12a, 17a, 19, 24-28

Early in the morning Samuel got up and went to meet Saul, but he was told, "Saul has gone to Carmel. There he has set up a monument in his own honor...."

Samuel said, "Although you were once small in your own eyes, did you not become the head of the tribes of Israel? ... Why did you not obey the LORD? Why did you pounce on the plunder and do evil in the eyes of the LORD?..."

Then Saul said to Samuel, "I have sinned. I violated the LORD's command and your instructions. I was afraid of the people and so I gave in to them. Now I beg you, forgive my sin and come back with me, so that I may worship the LORD."

But Samuel said to him, "I will not go back with you. You have rejected the word of the LORD, and the LORD has rejected you as king over Israel!"

As Samuel turned to leave, Saul caught hold of the hem of his robe, and it tore.

Samuel said to him, "The LORD has torn the kingdom of Israel from you today and has given it to one of your neighbors—to one better than you."

THE VOICE OF WISDOM

In the ancient world and through the Middle Ages, cities were fortified with walls against the potential attack of invading armies. Sometimes other barriers such as moats and pits were also constructed, but the walls of a city were its ultimate protection. A breach in the city's walls during a battle meant disaster, as the invaders poured into the city.

We, too, have walls like those ancient cities, and enemies who seek to break through the weak spots and destroy us. Do a complete self-inventory just as Nehemiah inventoried the walls of Jerusalem that had been broken down. And humbly submit to God's Spirit in prayer, asking for strength to reinforce those weaknesses.

What are the results of the breach of a personal wall? A witness for Christ is limited or destroyed. A life of service is hobbled or even shut down. The joy of purity is extinguished in guilt and sadness. Families are broken apart.

Watch your walls with care and prayer. Humble yourself before the living God. A breach in the walls can be devastating.

–AMY BEASLEY

Your best intentions are no match for the devil's trickery. But he gets weak in the knees when you lean on God.

DOWN IN FRONT

The spotlight isn't always very discriminating about who it shines on.
Careful leaders don't take its warmth to heart.

THE WORD FOR THE DAY

MOSES' MARRIAGE WAS JUST A CONVENIENT POINT OF ATTACK. WHEN A PERSON FEELS SLIGHTED, ANY EXCUSE TO POINT FINGERS WILL DO.

――― ❧ ―――

"HAS THE LORD SPOKEN ONLY THROUGH MOSES?" JEALOUS COMPARISONS WILL GET YOU INTO TROUBLE EVERY TIME.

――― ❧ ―――

"PROMOTION COMETH NEITHER FROM THE EAST, NOR FROM THE WEST, NOR FROM THE SOUTH. BUT GOD IS THE JUDGE: HE PUTTETH DOWN ONE, AND SETTETH UP ANOTHER"
(PSALM 75:6-7)

――― ❧ ―――

RECOGNITION USUALLY FINDS THOSE WHO DO THEIR WORK WELL.

Numbers 12:1-2, 4-7, 8b, 10a

Miriam and Aaron began to talk against Moses because of his Cushite wife, for he had married a Cushite.

"Has the LORD spoken only through Moses?" they asked. "Hasn't he also spoken through us?" And the LORD heard this....

At once the LORD said to Moses, Aaron and Miriam, "Come out to the Tent of Meeting, all three of you." So the three of them came out.

Then the LORD came down in a pillar of cloud, he stood at the entrance to the Tent and summoned Aaron and Miriam. When both of them stepped forward, he said, "Listen to my words. "When a prophet of the LORD is among you, I reveal myself to him in visions, I speak to him in dreams.

"But this is not true of my servant Moses; he is faithful in all my house.... Why then were you not afraid to speak against my servant Moses?..."

When the cloud lifted from above the Tent, there stood Miriam–leprous, like snow.

THE VOICE OF WISDOM

Leadership & Principle

NUMBER 16

TRUE LEADERS ARE UNSELFISH WITH THE LIMELIGHT.

She was a strong woman. Leadership came easily to her. And, as is often the case, this very strength became a weakness. Miriam, who had ascended to the highest post ever held by a woman, had surpassed her boundaries. She overestimated herself. She considered herself to be on the same level as Moses. And in her pride she undermined his authority. "Was he, indeed, the leader of the three of them?" she asked. "Weren't she and Aaron his equals?"

Miriam was not motivated by concern for the well-being of the people or for Moses, but by jealousy. Miriam was a woman at the top. It was an exceptional position, a commission which had been entrusted to her by God. However, Miriam gradually shifted away from God's control in her life to self control. This no doubt occurred so subtly that she didn't realize the change was taking place. Perhaps if she had searched her heart honestly in time, she could have prevented God's judgment. Perhaps then she would not have overstepped her boundaries by overestimating herself.

–GIEN KARSSEN

Be thankful for the kind words, but be sure to share the credit. Center stage isn't all it's cracked up to be.

CLOSER TO HOME

Your best chance at training leaders for tomorrow is to start by training the children who live under your own roof.

THE WORD FOR THE DAY

DAVID WASN'T PERFECT, AND HE FAILED HIS CHILDREN FAR TOO OFTEN BY HIS NEGLIGENCE, BUT HIS FINAL WORDS TO HIS SON ARE STRONG ONES: "WALK IN HIS WAYS."

―――――

USE ANY CHANCE YOU GET TO LET YOUR KIDS IN ON YOUR WORLD. IT WILL HELP YOU GROW TOGETHER, AND HELP THEM GROW THEIR STRENGTHS.

―――――

ARE YOUR CHILDREN ALWAYS WATCHING YOU LEAVE, OR GETTING TO WATCH FIRSTHAND HOW YOU LEAD?

―――――

YOU ARE RESPONSIBLE FOR HELPING YOUR CHILDREN'S LIVES BE "FIRMLY ESTABLISHED."

1 Kings 2:1-4, 10-12

When the time drew near for David to die, he gave a charge to Solomon his son.

"I am about to go the way of all the earth," he said. "So be strong, show yourself a man, and observe what the LORD your God requires: Walk in his ways, and keep his decrees and commands, his laws and requirements, as written in the Law of Moses, so that you may prosper in all you do and wherever you go, and that the LORD may keep his promise to me: 'If your descendants watch how they live, and if they walk faithfully before me with all their heart and soul, you will never fail to have a man on the throne of Israel. . . .'

Then David rested with his fathers and was buried in the City of David. He had reigned for forty years over Israel—seven years in Hebron and thirty-three in Jerusalem.

So Solomon sat on the throne of his father David, and his rule was firmly established.

THE VOICE OF WISDOM

Many professions—for example, doctors, nurses, therapists—require people to take a certain number of continuing education units per year to keep current with developments in their fields and to learn new skills. Even if you aren't in one of these professions, you probably have attended seminars or classes designed to teach you new procedures or help you make more efficient use of your time.

Sometimes you can kill two birds with one stone. I know a mother of three who's a physician specializing in family practice. When she went to a required continuing education seminar recently, her oldest son was about to turn thirteen. So she chose to attend a seminar about adolescent behavior and medical and psychological health in adolescence. This was material she needed for her job as a family doctor, but also for her job as a mom.

Choose educational opportunities that will allow you to learn for both careers at once. If your company sends you to a seminar, by all means learn the techniques for your job, but also think about how you can apply them at home.

–KATHY PEEL

You take your leadership skills for granted. But teach them to your children, so they can take them and run with them.

A FAIR ASSESSMENT

Authentic Christian leaders seek neither the spotlight nor the corner, but seek only the place God wants them to be.

YOUR ABILITIES ARE A GIFT FROM GOD, GIVEN FOR YOU TO USE, NOT TO APOLOGIZE FOR.

TRUE HUMILITY CALLS YOU TO UNDERSTAND EXACTLY WHERE YOU STAND WITH GOD— TOTALLY DEPENDENT, YET HIGHLY VALUABLE.

IF INSECURITY OR LACK OF CONFIDENCE KEEPS YOU FROM USING YOUR GIFTS, YOU'RE NOT WINNING BROWNIE POINTS FOR MEEKNESS. YOU ARE FAILING IN YOUR DUTY.

"EACH MEMBER BELONGS TO ALL THE OTHERS." EVEN THE LEADERSHIP GIFT IS A GIFT OF SERVICE.

Romans 12:2-8

Do not conform any longer to the pattern of this world, but be transformed by the renewing of your mind. Then you will be able to test and approve what God's will is–his good, pleasing and perfect will.

For by the grace given me I say to every one of you: Do not think of yourself more highly than you ought, but rather think of yourself with sober judgment, in accordance with the measure of faith God has given you.

Just as each of us has one body with many members, and these members do not all have the same function, so in Christ we who are many form one body, and each member belongs to all the others.

We have different gifts, according to the grace given us. If a man's gift is prophesying, let him use it in proportion to his faith. If it is serving, let him serve; if it is teaching, let him teach; if it is encouraging, let him encourage; if it is contributing to the needs of others, let him give generously; if it is leadership, let him govern diligently; if it is showing mercy, let him do it cheerfully.

THE VOICE OF WISDOM

God's acceptance of us in Christ Jesus is the fundamental truth upon which we build our lives. But if we ignore the necessity of self-acceptance, we render ourselves unable to take full advantage of the abundant life offered to us.

Yes, we need to acknowledge our weaknesses, to confess our sins. But if we want to be active, productive participants in the realm of God, we also need to recognize our gifts, to appreciate our strengths, to build on the abilities God has given us. We need to balance humility with confidence.

Flannery O'Connor, a brilliant writer and devout believer, was once asked why she became a writer. "Because I'm good at it," she replied. It was a statement of fact, not a declaration of arrogance. Self-acceptance is not pride. It is the proportional, "sober judgment" that allows us to see ourselves as we truly are, as God sees us.

Almighty God created us, redeemed us, called us, endowed us with gifts and abilities and perceptions. To demean the gift is to insult the Giver.

–PENELOPE STOKES

Leadership & Principle

NUMBER 18

GOOD LEADERS NEITHER THINK TOO HIGHLY NOR TOO LOWLY OF THEMSELVES.

Thank God for the myriad of talents He's invested in you. And thank Him more vividly by using them all well.

WHAT? ME, WORRY?

Tomorrow's meeting and next week's deadline are of little importance compared to what God wants you doing today.

THE WORD FOR THE DAY

RUTH DIDN'T GO INTO THE FIELDS SEEKING A HUSBAND, BUT GOD WAS WATCHING OUT FOR HER FUTURE NEEDS WHILE SHE WAS WATCHING AFTER HER DAILY TASKS.

GOD HAS A WAY OF WEAVING ALL YOUR PAST EXPERIENCES, RELATIONSHIPS, AND CONNECTIONS INTO A LIFE PLAN YOU NEVER WOULD HAVE FIGURED OUT ON YOUR OWN.

BE ON THE WATCH FOR "CHANCE" MEETINGS. GOD CAN MAKE GREAT THINGS DEVELOP FROM EVERYDAY MOMENTS.

ORDINARY OBEDIENCE IS THE ONLY REAL PATH TO FINDING GOD'S WILL.

Ruth 2:17, 19-23a

So Ruth gleaned in the field until evening. Then she threshed the barley she had gathered, and it amounted to about an ephah. . . .

Her mother-in-law asked her, "Where did you glean today? Where did you work? Blessed be the man who took notice of you!" Then Ruth told her mother-in-law about the one at whose place she had been working. "The name of the man I worked with today is Boaz," she said.

"The LORD bless him!" Naomi said to her daughter-in-law. "He has not stopped showing his kindness to the living and the dead." She added, "That man is our close relative; he is one of our kinsman-redeemers."

Then Ruth the Moabitess said, "He even said to me, 'Stay with my workers until they finish harvesting all my grain.'"

Naomi said to Ruth her daughter-in-law, "It will be good for you, my daughter, to go with his girls, because in someone else's field you might be harmed."

So Ruth stayed close to the servant girls of Boaz . . .

THE VOICE OF WISDOM

Leadership Principle

NUMBER 19

DO WHAT YOU OUGHT TO DO EACH DAY, AND TRUST GOD FOR THE RIGHT RESULTS.

Is it our business to pry into what may happen tomorrow? That is a difficult and painful exercise which saps the strength and uses up the time given us today. Once we give ourselves up to God, shall we attempt to get hold of what can never belong to us–tomorrow? Our lives are His, our times in His hand. He is Lord over what will happen, never mind what may happen. When we prayed, "Thy will be done," did we suppose He did not hear us? He heard indeed, and daily makes our business His and partakes of our lives. If my life is once surrendered, all is well. Let me not grab it back, as though it were in peril in His hand but would be safer in mine!

Today is mine. Tomorrow is none of my business. If I peer anxiously into the fog of the future, I will strain my spiritual eyes so that I will not see clearly what is required of me now.

"Sufficient unto the day is the evil thereof"–and the work thereof. The evil is not a part of the yoke Jesus asks us to take. Our work is, and He takes that yoke with us. I will overextend myself if I assume anything more.

–ELISABETH ELLIOT

If you can already see how you're going to get everything done, you're probably doing something too small.

THE BALANCING ACT

Your life as a leader will always push you beyond your own limits, but be careful that it doesn't push you over the edge.

THE WORD FOR THE DAY

THE CHURCH CAN OFTEN BE THE WORST AT EXPECTING MORE OF US THAN GOD HAS CALLED US TO SHOULDER. <u>NO</u> IS AN ACCEPTABLE ANSWER.

———— ❧ ————

A LIFE OUT OF BALANCE WILL EVENTUALLY ERUPT IN AN EXPLOSION OF BLAME, EXCUSES, AND FRUSTRATION.

———— ❧ ————

YOUR ABILITY TO COPE WITH RINGS OF RESPONSIBILITY WILL CAUSE PEOPLE TO ASK WHERE YOUR STRENGTH COMES FROM. INTRODUCE THEM TO YOUR SILENT PARTNER.

———— ❧ ————

"LET ME DO NOTHING TODAY WITHOUT CALMNESS OF SOUL."

—JOHN WESLEY

Luke 10:38-42
Matthew 6:31-33

As Jesus and his disciples were on their way, he came to a village where a woman named Martha opened her home to him. She had a sister called Mary, who sat at the Lord's feet listening to what he said.

But Martha was distracted by all the preparations that had to be made. She came to him and asked, "Lord, don't you care that my sister has left me to do the work by myself? Tell her to help me!"

"Martha, Martha," the Lord answered, "you are worried and upset about many things, but only one thing is needed. Mary has chosen what is better, and it will not be taken away from her."...

"So do not worry, saying, 'What shall we eat?' or 'What shall we drink?' or 'What shall we wear?' For the pagans run after all these things, and your heavenly Father knows that you need them.

"But seek first his kingdom and his righteousness, and all these things will be given to you as well."

THE VOICE OF WISDOM

God does not call us to be jugglers. God calls us to be people of balance. Martha, in the Bible, was an accomplished juggler. If she had lived in our generation, her last name probably would have been Stewart. When Jesus brought His disciples to her home, Martha scurried around fixing dinner, setting the table, creating a nice centerpiece, making sure everything was just perfect. Mary, Martha's sister didn't get in on the circus routine. Instead, she sat at the Master's feet and listened to what He was saying.

Finally, Martha began to lose her rhythm. Her juggling act was falling apart, and she panicked. "Lord," she said to Jesus, "don't you care that my sister has left me to do the work by myself? Tell her to help me! (Luke 10:40)

Does God care about all the responsibilities we have to juggle in our daily lives? Of course. But he cares more that our lives demonstrate balance, the ability to discern what is essential and give ourselves fully to it.

We may be able to juggle a lot of things at once, but we can only hold a few things at a time–our Lord, our loved ones, our inner lives, our outward calling.

–PENELOPE STOKES

Leadership Principle

NUMBER 20

KEEP YOURSELF IN CONSTANT BALANCE.

There's enough time today to do everything God expects. If you simply can't get it done, maybe it's not yours to do.

GOOD JOB, EVERYONE

You may be the one who gets the first round of applause.
But be quick to thank the others who deserve the acclaim.

THE WORD FOR THE DAY

PUBLIC STATEMENTS OF THANKS ARE NICE, BUT GOING OUT OF YOUR WAY TO SAY THANKS IN PRIVATE LETS PEOPLE KNOW YOU REALLY MEAN IT.

THANK-YOU NOTES SHOULD BE A STAPLE IN YOUR PURSE OR BRIEFCASE, SO YOU CAN SEIZE ANY SPARE MOMENT TO JOT A QUICK WORD OF GRATITUDE.

THE BEST WAY TO KEEP FROM SOUNDING PHONY IN YOUR PRAISE IS TO NOT BE. CULTIVATE A HEART OF GRATITUDE.

THOSE YOU BLESS AND CONGRATULATE WILL BE MORE RECEPTIVE TO YOUR OCCASIONAL REBUKE.

Philippians 4:10, 14-19

I rejoice greatly in the Lord that at last you have renewed your concern for me. Indeed, you have been concerned, but you had no opportunity to show it. . . .

Yet it was good of you to share in my troubles.

Moreover, as you Philippians know, in the early days of your acquaintance with the gospel, when I set out from Macedonia, not one church shared with me in the matter of giving and receiving, except you only; for even when I was in Thessalonica, you sent me aid again and again when I was in need.

Not that I am looking for a gift, but I am looking for what may be credited to your account. I have received full payment and even more; I am amply supplied, now that I have received from Epaphroditus the gifts you sent. They are a fragrant offering, an acceptable sacrifice, pleasing to God.

And my God will meet all your needs according to his glorious riches in Christ Jesus.

THE VOICE OF WISDOM

Leadership & Principle

NUMBER 21

WISE LEADERS EMPHASIZE THE CONTRIBUTIONS OF ALL THOSE INVOLVED IN THE ENDEAVOR.

Gratitude is a virtue we would do well to nurture. Life, after all, doesn't owe us happiness or contentment or personal fulfillment. These are not the source of gratitude but the results. We become happy, spiritually prosperous people not because we receive what we want, but because we appreciate what we have.

But gratitude doesn't end with our private thanks to God. We need to show gratitude as well to those who touch our lives.

The miracle of gratitude works both inside and out, backwards and forwards. As we express our gratefulness to the people who have given themselves to us, we minister to them and honor them for their faithfulness to God. But we also minister to ourselves. Gratitude tenderizes our hearts and makes us quicker to see and appreciate the daily gifts that come our way.

It's easy to take the gifts of life for granted, to accept them casually, as if we deserved God's generosity. But when we get a glimpse of the blessings that have been bestowed upon us, our hearts will overflow with gratitude, and our joy and contentment will spill over to those around us.

–PENELOPE STOKES

Commit to being a leader who notices people that others take for granted. Let them know you appreciate them.

THE TRUTH HELPS

The only way to know where you need to go—and to know how to get there—is to be honest about where you are now.

THE WORD FOR THE DAY

THE SPIES WEREN'T WRONG IN THEIR OBSERVATIONS, ONLY IN THEIR VISION.

———

OTHER PEOPLE OFTEN CAN'T SEE THE BIG PICTURE THE WAY YOU DO. AS A LEADER, YOU MUST SEE THE OBSTACLES, BUT WELCOME THE CHALLENGE.

———

JOSHUA AND CALEB HAD NO GUARANTEES THAT THEIR PLAN WOULD SUCCEED. WITH CONFIDENCE IN GOD, THEY WERE WILLING TO PUT THEIR LIVES ON THE LINE.

———

YOU'RE ASKING A LOT OF OTHERS. BE SURE YOU'RE WILLING TO GO RIGHT INTO THE FIGHT WITH THEM.

Numbers 14:2-4, 6-9

All the Israelites grumbled against Moses and Aaron, and the whole assembly said to them, "If only we had died in Egypt! Or in this desert! Why is the LORD bringing us to this land only to let us fall by the sword? Our wives and children will be taken as plunder. Wouldn't it be better for us to go back to Egypt?"

And they said to each other, "We should choose a leader and go back to Egypt. . . ."

Joshua son of Nun and Caleb son of Jephunneh, who were among those who had explored the land, tore their clothes and said to the entire Israelite assembly, "The land we passed through and explored is exceedingly good.

"If the LORD is pleased with us, he will lead us into that land, a land flowing with milk and honey, and will give it to us. Only do not rebel against the LORD. And do not be afraid of the people of the land, because we will swallow them up. Their protection is gone, but the LORD is with us. Do not be afraid of them."

THE VOICE OF WISDOM

At Webster Davis, you never heard children complaining to their teachers that such-and-such wasn't fair. We knew that such objections would get us nowhere. "Life is not fair," I heard many a teacher snap, " so don't go looking for fair." We accepted the inherent difficulties and injustices of life as we accepted the stifling humidity of Richmond summers. We didn't like it, and we stiffened our resolve to fight against it, but we conditioned ourselves to persevere and thrive in spite of it. And we knew with a knowing so deep that they must have seasoned the water fountains with it, that life was going to be tough. We never expected it to be easy. No one at Webster Davis, or in the black community at large, ever led us to believe that we could expect to get anything in life that we didn't sweat, bleed, and work for.

But even as our teachers painted us a realistic picture of black life in the fifties, they held up examples of those who had triumphed when the world was even more unfair. Their realism didn't discourage us. It encouraged us to succeed and flourish and overcome.

–KAY COLES JAMES

People will follow if you're honest about the problems, fair about the expectations, and confident about the outcome.

CONFRONTATIONS

*You are responsible for tending your vision and purpose—
and for dealing squarely with those who are endangering it.*

THE WORD FOR THE DAY

DEPENDING ON YOUR ARENA OF LEADERSHIP AND YOUR RELATIONSHIP WITH YOUR COWORKERS, YOU MAY NEED TO ADDRESS EVEN PERSONAL ISSUES OF CONCERN.

———— ❧ ————

THE YEAST PRINCIPLE SHOWS HOW EVEN A LITTLE DISCONTENT AMONG THE RANKS TENDS TO POISON OTHERS.

———— ❧ ————

"DO NOT JUDGE, OR YOU TOO WILL BE JUDGED" IS A TEACHING OF JESUS THAT SPEAKS TO PERSONAL INTEGRITY, BUT DOESN'T PRECLUDE US FROM PRACTICING OUR RIGHT—AND OUR NEED—TO JUDGE AND ADMONISH THOSE WITHIN OUR SPHERE OF RESPONSIBILITY.

1 Corinthians 5:1-2, 6, 9-12a

It is actually reported that there is sexual immorality among you, and of a kind that does not occur even among pagans: A man has his father's wife.

And you are proud! Shouldn't you rather have been filled with grief and have put out of your fellowship the man who did this?...

Your boasting is not good. Don't you know that a little yeast works through the whole batch of dough?...

I have written to you in my letter not to associate with sexually immoral people—not at all meaning the people of this world who are immoral, or the greedy and swindlers, or idolaters. In that case you would have to leave this world.

But now I am writing to you that you must not associate with anyone who calls himself a brother but is sexually immoral or greedy, an idolater or a slanderer, a drunkard or a swindler. With such a man do not even eat.

What business is it of mine to judge those outside the church? Are you not to judge those inside?

THE VOICE OF WISDOM

Leadership & Principle

NUMBER 23

LEADERS CANNOT BE AFRAID TO CONFRONT THOSE WHO ARE HARMING THE CAUSE.

To determine whether or not a situation is one that calls for confronting, ask yourself, "Why am I confronting?" It should not be to dump or unload your anger just to try to make you feel more comfortable. Nor should it be to lambaste others and put them in their place, or to punish, tear down, and get even.

Ask yourself these three significant questions: (1) Would it be for the good or the growth of the person; (2) for the good of the cause; (3) for the glory of God?

If you decide the issue is an important and legitimate one to confront, plan how you will lovingly do that.

Carefully consider the right time to confront. It should be after you have identified and clarified the real issue. It should be after you have examined your own heart for any fleshly motives that might be causing your hurt, anger, or disappointment. It should be after you know assuredly that this is God's way and time for you to address the situation and after you have cooled enough to do it with grace and truth, to take the emotion out of it. Confronting should be done before the issue grows too large.

–VERNA BIRKEY

Is there someone whose work and attitude is draining the life out of others on your team? Consider the consequences.

THOUGHTFUL OF YOU

*There's work to be done and only so much time to do it,
but caring for those around you should be business as usual.*

THE WORD FOR THE DAY

THE PRIEST AND THE LEVITE SURELY HAD WELL-WORDED RATIONALES FOR PASSING UP THE MAN IN NEED. YOU MAY HAVE HEARD THEM PASSING THROUGH YOUR OWN MIND A TIME OR TWO.

―――― ⟨✺⟩ ――――

WHEREVER POSSIBLE, PLAN SOME AIR INTO YOUR DAY. YOU NEVER KNOW WHEN SOMETHING MORE IMPORTANT MIGHT COME UP.

―――― ⟨✺⟩ ――――

ONE HAND-WRITTEN NOTE (JUST A SHORT ONE) CAN DO MORE THAN A DOZEN ENCOURAGING WORDS OR PHONE CALLS.

―――― ⟨✺⟩ ――――

JESUS SAID, "GO AND DO LIKEWISE." YES, THAT MEANS US.

Luke 10:30-34, 36-37

In reply Jesus said: "A man was going down from Jerusalem to Jericho, when he fell into the hands of robbers. They stripped him of his clothes, beat him and went away, leaving him half dead.

"A priest happened to be going down the same road, and when he saw the man, he passed by on the other side.

"So too, a Levite, when he came to the place and saw him, passed by on the other side.

"But a Samaritan, as he traveled, came where the man was; and when he saw him, he took pity on him.

"He went to him and bandaged his wounds, pouring on oil and wine. Then he put the man on his own donkey, brought him to an inn and took care of him. . . .

"Which of these three do you think was a neighbor to the man who fell into the hands of robbers?"

The expert in the law replied, "The one who had mercy on him." Jesus told him, "Go and do likewise."

THE VOICE OF WISDOM

There are times when interruptions should be treated as opportunities. Jesus accomplished His purpose and never appeared to be without time for unscheduled interruptions. In one biblical example, He was on His way to see Jairus' sick daughter. He must have been focused on His goal, arriving before the sick girl died. But Jesus was interrupted by another one in need–not a ruler's child at the point of death, but an unclean, chronically ill woman. Jesus lovingly and patiently took the time to heal the woman and to bless her. He turned the interruption into an opportunity.

In *The Time Minder*, Ruth Miller says that interruptions can be viewed in one of two ways: either as annoying, frustrating blockades to our best-laid plans or as God's little nudges. Similarly, Charles W. Shedd in *Time for All Things* refers to "divine interruptions." He concludes that one of the marks of Christian greatness is a certain interruptability.

Our life should have an elastic quality with room for one more real need if it comes from higher up.

–DEBBIE LLOYD

Leadership & Principle

NUMBER 24

TAKING THE TIME TO BE THOUGHTFUL OF OTHERS SEPARATES GOOD LEADERS FROM GREAT ONES.

You'll have some unplanned opportunities to be unusually kind today. Why don't you make that part of your plan?

THE BIBLE TELLS ME SO

*People can hide big questions beneath the surface of their small talk.
Are you prepared to offer the answers of faith?*

THE WORD FOR THE DAY

THE WITNESS OF YOUR CHARACTER WILL CREATE OPPORTUNITIES FOR THE WITNESS OF YOUR WORDS.
BE READY TO RESPOND.

———— ❧ ————

"ALWAYS BE PREPARED TO GIVE AN ANSWER TO EVERYONE WHO ASKS YOU TO GIVE THE REASON FOR THE HOPE THAT YOU HAVE" (1 PETER 3:15).

———— ❧ ————

GET TO KNOW THE KIND OF QUESTIONS THAT CUT THROUGH THE CLUTTER, THE ONES THAT OPEN PEOPLE'S HEARTS TO HEAR WHAT YOU HAVE TO SAY.

———— ❧ ————

TRY TO DISCERN WHAT PEOPLE ARE REALLY ASKING, SO YOUR TESTIMONY CAN SPEAK TO THEM RIGHT WHERE THEY ARE.

Acts 8:26-31, 34-35

Now an angel of the Lord said to Philip, "Go south to the road—the desert road—that goes down from Jerusalem to Gaza."

So he started out, and on his way he met an Ethiopian eunuch, an important official in charge of all the treasury of Candace, queen of the Ethiopians. This man had gone to Jerusalem to worship,

and on his way home was sitting in his chariot reading the book of Isaiah the prophet.

The Spirit told Philip, "Go to that chariot and stay near it." Then Philip ran up to the chariot and heard the man reading Isaiah the prophet. "Do you understand what you are reading?" Philip asked.

"How can I," he said, "unless someone explains it to me?" So he invited Philip to come up and sit with him. . . .

The eunuch asked Philip, "Tell me, please, who is the prophet talking about, himself or someone else?" Then Philip began with that very passage of Scripture and told him the good news about Jesus.

THE VOICE OF WISDOM

I believe that God's purpose for me, day by day and moment by moment, is to direct me to be more like Jesus. I believe that because I am called by God to that purpose, all things will work together for good. I believe that in expressing that belief, I am called to live it out when I encounter crisis or challenge. I believe that God would never call me to a purpose for which he would not empower me.

I believe in the indwelling Holy Spirit, who stirs, comforts, and fills me as I live in this flesh. I believe in the fellowship of that Spirit with other believers.

I believe in forgiveness. The more I come to know my forgiven self, the more I believe in the restorative power of the good news of forgiveness. I believe we miss much when we forgive little.

I believe that believers make a difference in the world. I believe we make that difference by loving well and living in hope. I believe God is able to handle the results of every life that I touch today. I believe that because I believe, life is wonderfully beautiful and deeply mysterious. I believe, and I will press on.

–LINDA PAGE

Leadership & Principle

NUMBER 25

CHRISTIAN LEADERS SHOULD NOT ONLY LIVE THEIR FAITH, BUT KNOW HOW TO PUT IT INTO WORDS.

As you read the Bible, try to look beyond what it's saying to you and consider how God can help you speak it to others.

A WORD FITLY SPOKEN

*Every day you meet people who need your encouragement,
your help, your insight, your time. Are you giving it?*

THE WORD FOR THE DAY

CHRISTIAN LEADERS SHOULD HAVE ALL THE MOTIVATION THEY NEED TO ACTIVELY SEEK WAYS TO HELP THOSE AROUND THEM: "FOR CHRIST'S LOVE COMPELS US."

———— ❧ ————

"FROM NOW ON WE REGARD NO ONE FROM A WORLDLY POINT OF VIEW." WORK HARD TO SEE PEOPLE'S POTENTIAL RATHER THAN THEIR PAST.

———— ❧ ————

IF YOU WERE A PERSON UNDER YOUR LEADERSHIP, HOW WOULD YOU LIKE TO BE TREATED?

———— ❧ ————

EVEN IF YOUR WORKPLACE DOESN'T BELIEVE IT, REMEMBER THAT PEOPLE'S GREATEST NEED IS THEIR NEED FOR JESUS.

2 Corinthians 5:14-20

For Christ's love compels us, because we are convinced that one died for all, and therefore all died.

And he died for all, that those who live should no longer live for themselves but for him who died for them and was raised again.

So from now on we regard no one from a worldly point of view. Though we once regarded Christ in this way, we do so no longer.

Therefore, if anyone is in Christ, he is a new creation; the old has gone, the new has come!

All this is from God, who reconciled us to himself through Christ and gave us the ministry of reconciliation: that God was reconciling the world to himself in Christ, not counting men's sins against them. And he has committed to us the message of reconciliation.

We are therefore Christ's ambassadors, as though God were making his appeal through us. We implore you on Christ's behalf: Be reconciled to God.

THE VOICE OF WISDOM

People helping people is what life is all about, whether it takes the form of encouraging, mentoring, or counseling. In fact, God's whole redemptive purpose is wrapped up in the word *reconciliation*.

The overall goal in helping any individual is to communicate hope, that they might more courageously and confidently face daily life with its trials and struggles. Our God is a God of hope: "May the God of hope fill you with all joy and peace as you trust in him, so that you may overflow with hope by the power of the Holy Spirit" (Romans 15:13).

God gives hope to His children through a sense of His presence, through the numberless promises in His Word, and through His gracious, generous provisions–including the loving, caring, and understanding members of His church body.

We need to communicate that hope and encourage others to "hope against hope" as Abraham did. When hope was dead within him, he went on hoping in faith, believing that he would become "the father of many nations" (Romans 4:18).

–VERNA BIRKEY

Leadership Principle

NUMBER 26

EFFECTIVE LEADERS GET PERSONALLY INVOLVED TO SOLVE DIFFICULT PERSONAL PROBLEMS.

The easiest course of action is to not get involved. But by making yourself vulnerable, you make yourself valuable.

A PARENT'S PRIORITY

As hard as it is to admit, we can all be replaced.
But not as the parents of our children. We're all that they've got.

THE WORD FOR THE DAY

TRAINING YOUR CHILDREN TO OBEY YOU NOW WILL MAKE IT THAT MUCH EASIER FOR THEM TO OBEY GOD LATER.

———— ❧ ————

MAKE TIME TO TALK. AND ALSO TO LISTEN.

———— ❧ ————

HOW WELL DO YOUR KIDS KNOW YOUR LIFE STORY? THEY CAN LEARN A LOT FROM WHAT GOD'S DONE WITH YOU.

———— ❧ ————

GODLY CHILDREN ARE THE BEST INVESTMENT YOU CAN MAKE IN LIFE.

———— ❧ ————

IF YOU CAN'T EXPLAIN YOUR BELIEFS WHERE A CHILD CAN UNDERSTAND, YOU MAY NOT UNDERSTAND THEM ALL THAT WELL YOURSELF.

Psalm 78:1-8

O my people, hear my teaching; listen to the words of my mouth.

I will open my mouth in parables, I will utter hidden things, things from of old—what we have heard and known, what our fathers have told us.

We will not hide them from their children; we will tell the next generation the praiseworthy deeds of the LORD, his power, and the wonders he has done.

He decreed statutes for Jacob and established the law in Israel, which he commanded our forefathers to teach their children, so that the next generation would know them, even the children yet to be born, and they in turn would tell their children.

Then they would put their trust in God and would not forget his deeds but would keep his commands.

They would not be like their forefathers—a stubborn and rebellious generation, whose hearts were not loyal to God, whose spirits were not faithful to him.

THE VOICE OF WISDOM

Being a successful mother does not depend on whether you work outside the home or not. I want to encourage the working mothers reading this, especially those who have no choice, that you can be the mother God wants you to be, and your children can have the attention and nurturing they need. You and your children are not doomed for failure just because you work.

But there is a price to pay. And for working moms, it means giving a lot of yourself, of your time and energy. Time that you might prefer to spend quietly reading, time when you would like to go to bed early, or time when you really didn't want to go to a school function after working all day. These are the sacrifices that are very real for working moms.

The most important thing you can do is pour prayer time into this situation. A praying mom, one whose life is absolutely on track with the Lord, who spends time in His Word, and lives it before her children is what your children need. You can be that kind of mom, whether you work outside your home or not.

–MARY WHELCHEL

> *Leadership & Principle*
>
> NUMBER 27
>
> NO MATTER HOW IMPORTANT YOUR ROLE, PARENTING YOUR CHILDREN IS MORE IMPORTANT.

What's keeping you from giving your best to your children? And is it worth the price you're paying to keep it there?

WHO KNOWS?

*Perhaps the best thing you can know is that you can't know everything—
but that you serve a living God who does.*

THE WORD FOR THE DAY

MOST OF US CAN BE REALLY
GOOD AT ONLY A FEW THINGS.
TRYING TO DO TOO MUCH CAN
ONLY DILUTE AND WEAKEN
YOUR STRENGTHS.

———— ✍ ————

NEVER BE AFRAID TO SAY "I
DON'T KNOW."

———— ✍ ————

AS A CHRISTIAN, YOU CAN
REST IN THE FACT THAT THE
HOLY SPIRIT IN YOU CAN
BUBBLE UP ETERNAL WISDOM
AT A MOMENT'S NOTICE—
RIGHT WHEN YOU NEED IT.

———— ✍ ————

JUST BECAUSE YOUR PLAN
DOESN'T RECEIVE IMMEDIATE
CONSENSUS DOESN'T NECESSAR-
ILY MEAN YOU'RE WRONG.
GIVE IDEAS TIME TO GROW
AND DEVELOP.

1 Corinthians 2:1-7, 9-10

When I came to you, brothers, I did not come with eloquence or superior wisdom as I proclaimed to you the testimony about God.

For I resolved to know nothing while I was with you except Jesus Christ and him crucified. I came to you in weakness and fear, and with much trembling.

My message and my preaching were not with wise and persuasive words, but with a demonstration of the Spirit's power, so that your faith might not rest on men's wisdom, but on God's power.

We do, however, speak a message of wisdom among the mature, but not the wisdom of this age or of the rulers of this age, who are coming to nothing.

No, we speak of God's secret wisdom, a wisdom that has been hidden and that God destined for our glory before time began. . . . as it is written: "No eye has seen, no ear has heard, no mind has conceived what God has prepared for those who love him"–but God has revealed it to us by his Spirit.

THE VOICE OF WISDOM

Even before mentoring came along, Henry L. Mencken observed: "The older I get, the more I distrust the familiar doctrine that age brings wisdom."

Our first step toward gaining God's wisdom is to know what we do not know; that is, to be aware of our shortcomings. The apostle Paul, in 1 Corinthians 2, assured the church members of Corinth that he hadn't dared to show up to preach among them armed only with his glowing wit and wisdom. In fact, he feared and trembled with awareness of his own shortcomings. The method, as well as the results there, was God's effort. Therefore, because it was God's wisdom he shared, he had every confidence that the effects of his visit would last.

We, too, have come to the realization that all the printouts in the world, all the marketing plans by the best corporate planning departments, and all the technical experts available to us do not have all the answers. Saying that we recognize these limitations is one thing; believing it is something else again.

–DIANNA BOOHER

Leadership & Principle

NUMBER 28

LEADERS REALIZE THEY CAN'T KNOW EVERYTHING ABOUT EVERYTHING.

Questions are allowed. Ask them often. But ultimately, you must take action using the best information you have.

PEACE OF HIS MIND

*Trusting God to accomplish His will through your work makes
you no less responsible, just a lot less irritable.*

THE WORD FOR THE DAY

YOU MAY HAVE LONELY DECISIONS TO MAKE, BUT YOU HAVE "A FRIEND WHO STICKS CLOSER THAN A BROTHER" (PROVERBS 18:24).

———— ❧ ————

RELAX—GOD IS ALWAYS ON THE JOB.

———— ❧ ————

PEACE OF MIND DOES NOT COME FROM DOING EVERYTHING PERFECTLY, BUT FROM TRUSTING GOD TO WORK THROUGH YOU.

———— ❧ ————

PEACE IS NOT THE ABSENCE OF CONFLICT, BUT THE ABILITY TO STAY AT REST AMID CONFLICT.

———— ❧ ————

GOD PROMISES PEACE THAT "TRANSCENDS ALL UNDERSTANDING" (PHILIPPIANS 4:7).

*Isaiah 40:27-31
Psalm 37:39-40*

Why do you say, O Jacob, and complain, O Israel, "My way is hidden from the LORD; my cause is disregarded by my God"?

Do you not know? Have you not heard? The LORD is the everlasting God, the Creator of the ends of the earth. He will not grow tired or weary, and his understanding no one can fathom.

He gives strength to the weary and increases the power of the weak.

Even youths grow tired and weary, and young men stumble and fall; but those who hope in the LORD will renew their strength. They will soar on wings like eagles; they will run and not grow weary, they will walk and not be faint. . . .

The salvation of the righteous comes from the LORD; he is their stronghold in time of trouble.

The LORD helps them and delivers them; he delivers them from the wicked and saves them, because they take refuge in him.

THE VOICE OF WISDOM

Strong women intrigue me. I enjoy watching them organize large fund-raisers that make life better for less fortunate individuals. I admire parenting skills that strong women use; they work carefully to empower their children and help them grow strong. The world is a good place because of sensitive, strong women.

But when is strength really a weakness? I have to admit that when it comes to the big decisions of life, trusting God is not my first line of thought. Instinctively, I look within myself for answers.

How often I make my plans and ask for God's blessing on my plan. Then with jaw set I move ahead thinking that my will is His will–which finds me, again and again, needing to return to my point of departure and seek His wisdom on the front end of a decision.

Trusting God does not make me less of a woman. It doesn't compromise my personality as a strong woman. Depending on Him celebrates the wonderful, miraculous gift He has entrusted to me. Trusting Him is my strength.

–SUZANNE DALE EZELL

Leadership & Principle

NUMBER 29

TRUSTING GOD RESULTS IN PEACE OF MIND.

Feeling the weight of the world on your shoulders? Trust your troubles to One who's worth His weight in wisdom.

CHURCH SERVICE

The church may already be your arena of leadership.
But we all have a responsibility to pull our weight in this family.

THE WORD FOR THE DAY

FAITHFULNESS IN YOUR CHURCH LIFE WILL VALIDATE YOUR PUBLIC LIFE.

⎯⎯ ∽ ⎯⎯

THE BIBLE INDICATES THAT THOSE WITH GREATER RESPONSIBILITIES ARE HELD TO A HIGHER LEVEL OF ACCOUNTABILITY. DON'T COMPARE YOUR CONTRIBUTIONS WITH OTHERS'.

⎯⎯ ∽ ⎯⎯

"LET US CONSIDER . . . ONE ANOTHER." ONE OF THE MAIN REASONS WE NEED OUR CHURCH IS TO TAKE OUR ATTENTION OFF OUR OWN NEEDS.

⎯⎯ ∽ ⎯⎯

LEADERSHIP MAY COME EASY TO YOU, BUT IT DOESN'T TO EVERYONE. ARE YOU LETTING GOD USE YOUR LEADERSHIP GIFT—AND ALL YOUR GIFTS— IN MINISTRY?

Hebrews 10:19-25
1 Corinthians 12:12

Therefore, brothers, since we have confidence enter the Most Holy Place by the blood of Jesus, *a new and living way opened for us through t* curtain, that is, his body, and since we have *great priest over the house of God, let us dra* near to God with a sincere heart in full assuran *of faith, having our hearts sprinkled to cleanse* from a guilty conscience and having our bodi *washed with pure water.*

Let us hold unswervingly to the hope we pr fess, for he who promised is faithful.

And let us consider how we may spur on another on towards love and good deeds.

Let us not give up meeting together, as some a in the habit of doing, but let us encourage on another—and all the more as you see the Da *approaching. . . .*

The body is a unit, though it is made up many parts; and though all its parts are man *they form one body. So it is with Christ.*

THE VOICE OF WISDOM

The question of our role in Christ's body demands our attention. God never called us to be spectators. He called us to be participants. We unite with believers to know and do the will and work of God. He never intended for us to function alone.

We know that we are to join with Christ's body because He instructs us to do so. When we believe on and receive Jesus Christ, we become a permanent part of God's family. Participation is not optional. God designed His body for our personal well-being and to ensure effectiveness in our mission to the world.

When a united group has like goals, common purposes are achieved. So we join with God's people to grow in our knowledge of Him, to be encouraged in our faith, and to receive needed support individually and as a body to accomplish His will in our generation.

The mission of the church, simply stated, is threefold–evangelize, assimilate, and nurture. How well is your church fulfilling its calling? How well are you contributing to its success? How effectively are you investing yourself in Christ's ministry?

–LINDA MCGINN

When you write out your tithe check this week, ask yourself whether you've tithed your time to the Lord, as well.

WORK YOUR PLAN

*The time you spend in putting legs, arms, and feet on your vision
will be the best investment you make as a leader.*

THE WORD FOR THE DAY

NEHEMIAH GOT HIS BIG BREAK
BECAUSE HE WAS READY WITH
AN ANSWER TO THE KING'S
OFF-HAND QUESTION.

———— ❧ ————

SEVEN OTHER TIMES THE BIBLE
MENTIONS NEHEMIAH'S PRAY-
ING. THAT'S WHERE PLANNING
SHOULD START.

———— ❧ ————

HE WASN'T AFRAID TO ASK
FOR EVEN MORE THAN HE
REALLY EXPECTED TO GET.

———— ❧ ————

PART OF NEHEMIAH'S PLAN
WAS TO PLAN FOR OPPOSITION.

———— ❧ ————

ABOVE ALL, HE KNEW THAT
THE SUCCESS OF HIS UNDER-
TAKING DEPENDED
TOTALLY ON GOD.

Nehemiah 2:4-8

The king said to me, "What is it you want?"
Then I prayed to the God of heaven, and
answered the king, "If it pleases the king and i
your servant has found favor in his sight, let hin
send me to the city in Judah where my fathers ar
buried so that I can rebuild it."

Then the king, with the queen sitting besid
him, asked me, "How long will your journey take
and when will you get back?" It pleased the kin
to send me; so I set a time.

I also said to him, "If it pleases the king, may
have letters to the governors of Trans-Euphrates
so that they will provide me safe-conduct until
arrive in Judah?

"And may I have a letter to Asaph, keeper of th
king's forest, so he will give me timber to make
beams for the gates of the citadel by the templ
and for the city wall and for the residence I wil
occupy?" And because the gracious hand of my
God was upon me, the king granted my requests.

THE VOICE OF WISDOM

A franchising consultant once told me, "A good idea is worth one dollar. The plan for implementing that idea is worth a million dollars." What good does it do to stir up a crowd if you do not give them a constructive outlet for their energy?

A good leader has a plan that consists of simple pictures. Just because a group of people has a bunch of boards, hammers, and nails does not mean that they are building a house or even anything recognizable. Sometimes leaders think they are doing their job just because there is a lot of hammering going on.

Sometimes a plan can start with one simple objective. The civil rights movement was constructed around singular objectives. Sometimes they were as simple as: Make sure blacks do not have to sit at the back of the bus. *Equal rights* is an intangible idea. It is hard for people to grasp a concept that does not have pictures attached to it. Being forced to sit in the back of the bus creates a picture that people can get excited, angry, or motivated about. The desire to change that picture evolved into a plan.

–LAURIE BETH JONES

Leadership Principle

NUMBER 31

PROPER PLANNING CAN HELP YOU AVOID MOST OF YOUR MISTAKES.

Before you take another step in the wrong direction, back up to where you started. And start off again with a plan.

SINGLE MINDED

*It's only when you truly know what your driving purpose is
that you can steer your life in the direction God desires.*

THE WORD FOR THE DAY

JESUS KNEW EXACTLY WHO HE WAS. THAT FACT MADE HIM ABLE TO ORDER HIS EARTHLY LIFE BENEATH HIS PURPOSE AND PRIORITIES.

———— ✎ ————

OTHERS MAY NOT ALWAYS UNDERSTAND WHY YOU DO WHAT YOU DO, WHY YOU MUST SOMETIMES SAY NO TO THE FUN AND FLEETING.

———— ✎ ————

IT IS HELPFUL AT TIMES TO PUT YOUR PRIORITIES ON PAPER, AND TO REFER TO THEM DOWN THE ROAD TO SEE IF YOU'RE STAYING ON TRACK.

———— ✎ ————

ARE YOUR LIFE'S GOALS DEFINED BY YOUR RELATIONSHIP WITH JESUS? IF NOT, YOU SHOULD MAKE NEW ONES.

John 8:13-14, 25-29

The Pharisees challenged him, "Here you are, appearing as your own witness; your testimony is not valid."

Jesus answered, "Even if I testify on my own behalf, my testimony is valid, for I know where I came from and where I am going. But you have no idea where I come from or where I am going. . . .

"Who are you?" they asked. "Just what I have been claiming all along," Jesus replied. "I have much to say in judgment of you. But he who sent me is reliable, and what I have heard from him I tell the world."

They did not understand that he was telling them about his Father.

So Jesus said, "When you have lifted up the Son of Man, then you will know that I am the one I claim to be and that I do nothing on my own but speak just what the Father has taught me.

"The one who sent me is with me; he has not left me alone, for I always do what pleases him."

THE VOICE OF WISDOM

Thank God I know–knew from a very early age–the work I was born to do. For me, writing is less a profession than a compulsion. A calling. Calling–what a lovely word, fraught with so much meaning. For inner voices do call, sometimes faintly, sometimes fiercely, "Come, come, follow me."

Leadership & Principle

NUMBER 32

KNOW WHAT YOUR PURPOSE IS, AND MAKE SURE YOUR ACTIVITIES LINE UP UNDERNEATH IT.

Of course a lot of little voices try to join the chorus. We get diverted, race this direction, that. But there is no denying the true voice; our very soul recognizes it, and there will be no peace unless we heed.

There is something more, though. There is dedication. A sense of commitment to your work so great you will endure great sacrifices for it, give it your all and a little bit more. If your work is truly vital to you, then you will pour yourself into it, body, soul, and blood. Not to compete with anybody, nor for the money, nor for acclaim, but out of a sense of fulfilling your personal mission, your God-given purpose. And far from separating you from God, it will be a form of worship. Of knowing you are truly one with him and he is one with you.

–MARJORIE HOLMES

Do you have a feel for God's will? Do you know where you're going? Will you know it when you get there?

OK, WHAT'S NEXT?

Adversity is a main course in the leader's diet.
And the best way to swallow it is to eat everything that's on your plate.

"BUT JONAH RAN AWAY FROM THE LORD." RUNNING FROM YOUR PROBLEMS ONLY MAKES THEM GROW STRONGER.

———— ❧ ————

TRY TACKLING YOUR HARDEST TASKS FIRST, RATHER THAN DREADING THEM ALL DAY.

———— ❧ ————

IF YOUR MAIN SOURCE OF ADVERSITY IS OTHER PEOPLE, LEARN THE FINE ART OF BEING GENTLE BUT DIRECT, CALM BUT CLEAR. AS HARD AS IT IS NOW, IT WILL ONLY GET WORSE IF YOU LET THINGS GO.

———— ❧ ————

GOD GAVE JONAH A SECOND CHANCE. HE KNOWS THIS IS A TOUGH ONE. JUST KEEP TRYING.

Jonah 1:1-4, 10, 11b, 15, 17

The word of the LORD came to Jonah son of Amittai: "Go to the great city of Nineveh and preach against it, because its wickedness has come up before me."

But Jonah ran away from the LORD and headed for Tarshish. He went down to Joppa, where he found a ship bound for that port. After paying the fare, he went aboard and sailed for Tarshish to flee from the LORD.

Then the LORD sent a great wind on the sea, and such a violent storm arose that the ship threatened to break up.

This terrified them and they asked, "What have you done?" (They knew he was running away from the LORD, because he had already told them so.) ... So they asked him, "What should we do to you to make the sea calm down for us?" ...

Then they took Jonah and threw him overboard, and the raging sea grew calm. ...

But the LORD provided a great fish to swallow Jonah, and Jonah was inside the fish three days and three nights.

THE VOICE OF WISDOM

Waves of crisis or difficulty roll in from the horizon and threaten to break over my life. Looking up at them, they seem so high, so insurmountable. My first inclination is to run the other way, fleeing from those frightening problems. But I've learned that there is no fast escape. Running from problems only tosses me in a foaming fury of entanglements and frustrations and emotions later on.

Jonah learned that lesson in a tough college course called Obedience 101. When he tried to run from the clear challenge God had laid before him, life became exceedingly complicated.

Jonah would agree with me that the best way to beat these waves of trials and tough challenges is to face them. Head on. Almost anticipating them. Sometimes I find myself literally diving into the middle of a problem before it has a chance to crash on top of me.

And when by God's grace I come through it all? Oh, the relief when I know that problem is behind me. With God's help, I've beaten it. What an invigorating feeling!

–JONI EARECKSON TADA

Leadership & Principle

NUMBER 33

LEADERS SHOULD NOT SEEK ADVERSITY, BUT SHOULDN'T RUN FROM IT EITHER.

You may have tried everything you know to conquer a nagging problem. Have you asked God for an action plan?

TALKING POINTS

Communication can be talking, listening, whatever.
But one thing's for sure. Communication better be happening.

THE WORD FOR THE DAY

ONE OF THE BIGGEST OBSTACLES TO SUCCESSFUL COMMUNICATION IS NOT KNOWING EXACTLY WHAT YOU'RE TRYING TO SAY. DON'T EXPECT OTHERS TO UNDERSTAND SOMETHING YOU DON'T QUITE UNDERSTAND YOURSELF.

—————— ❧ ——————

WHAT MAY SEEM LIKE A LACK OF EFFORT MAY REALLY BE A LACK OF CONFIDENCE. WHEN DEBORAH SAW IT FORMING IN BARAK, SHE CAME ALONGSIDE TO WALK HIM THROUGH IT.

—————— ❧ ——————

ARE YOU COMMUNICATING CLEAR GOALS AND MEASURABLE REWARDS? PEOPLE LIKE TO SEE THAT WHAT THEY'RE DOING IS MAKING A DIFFERENCE.

Judges 4:4-9

Deborah, a prophetess, the wife of Lappidoth, was leading Israel at that time. She held court under the Palm of Deborah between Ramah and Bethel in the hill country of Ephraim, and the Israelites came to her to have their disputes decided.

She sent for Barak son of Abinoam from Kedesh in Naphtali and said to him, "The LORD, the God of Israel, commands you: 'Go, take with you ten thousand men of Naphtali and Zebulun and lead the way to Mount Tabor.

"I will lure Sisera, the commander of Jabin's army, with his chariots and his troops to the Kishon River and give him into your hands.'"

Barak said to her, "If you go with me, I will go, but if you don't go with me, I won't go."

"Very well," Deborah said, "I will go with you. But because of the way you are going about this, the honor will not be yours, for the LORD will hand Sisera over to a woman."

THE VOICE OF WISDOM

Deborah is a woman who demonstrates the very best principles of an approach called situational leadership. Taking into account the needs of the people she was leading, she changed her style in order to help them grow in the tasks she assigned them. This can give us guidance regarding the communication style to use in a given situation.

Leaders can't be leaders, after all, if their followers don't follow them! That means leaders must be carefully tuned in to the needs of their followers.

If a leader meets a person's needs, that person will be extremely loyal. Too often leaders begin to think that followers are supposed to meet the leader's needs. And at that point, the leader will begin to lose strength as a leader.

There is no one perfect leadership or communication style. And no leader is perfect. But the most effective leaders remember that people perform best when their needs are met. A good leader asks questions and listens carefully to assure that she can offer the direction and support most needed by her team.

–HARRIET HARRAL

Leadership & *Principle*

NUMBER 34

EFFECTIVE LEADERS KEEP THEIR LINES OF COMMUNICATION OPEN, CLEAR, AND HONEST.

When problems arise between you and others under your authority, ask yourself a question: Am I communicating?

DO UNTO OTHERS

There's not a decision you'll make today that can't be run through the Golden Rule filter. What would Jesus do?

THE WORD FOR THE DAY

THE HARDEST THINGS TO DO AND THE EASIEST THINGS TO FORGET ARE SOMETIMES THE SIMPLEST AND MOST BASIC.

———— ⤫ ————

LETTING BIBLICAL PRINCIPLES GUIDE YOUR LEADERSHIP TASKS GIVES YOU EXAMPLES TO SHARE WITH OTHERS ABOUT HOW GOD'S WORD APPLIES TO DAILY LIFE.

———— ⤫ ————

JESUS TOOK TIME TO HEAR AND ENCOURAGE THIS ONE WHO WAS TRULY SEEKING HIM. HE KNOWS YOUR HEART.

———— ⤫ ————

YOU NEED NO OTHER EXPLANATION THAN THIS FOR ONE OF YOUR LEADERSHIP ACTIONS: "IT'S A GOLDEN RULE THING."

Mark 12:28–34a

One of the teachers of the law came and heard them debating. Noticing that Jesus had given them a good answer, he asked him, "Of all the commandments, which is the most important?"

"The most important one," answered Jesus, "is this: 'Hear, O Israel, the Lord our God, the Lord is one. Love the Lord your God with all your heart and with all your soul and with all your mind and with all your strength.'

The second is this: 'Love your neighbor as yourself.' There is no commandment greater than these."

"Well said, teacher," the man replied. "You are right in saying that God is one and there is no other but him. To love him with all your heart, with all your understanding and with all your strength, and to love your neighbor as yourself is more important than all burnt offerings and sacrifices."

When Jesus saw that he had answered wisely, he said to him, "You are not far from the kingdom of God."

THE VOICE OF WISDOM

I need to agree with Jesus when he puts my actions under the microscope. One day, I was at the home of a new friend. We were talking about life and ministry, and our conversation slipped over into commenting on someone's life over which we had no influence. As I walked from her house, the Holy Spirit convicted me of my sin of gossip. I tried to rationalize it. *God, I'm a leader. I can't apologize for something this petty–she might lose respect for me. God, what if I do apologize and she feels I'm judging her? She might not want to be my friend. Really, Lord, it wasn't that big of a deal–we were just sharing our convictions.* But as I walked, I knew I had to call her as soon as I got home, and I had to leave the results to God.

"Jenna, I just had to call and tell you I'm sorry for the things I said about Margaret. It wasn't my place to say them, and I am sorry for dragging you into the conversation."

"Pam, I was feeling the same way, and I was just standing here deciding whether I should call you." Our friendship was cemented that day because I agreed with Jesus.

–PAM FARREL

Leadership & Principle

NUMBER 35

DO TO OTHERS AS YOU WOULD HAVE THEM DO TO YOU.

What rules are defining your daily choices? Try putting on paper the godly guidelines that you want driving you.

A SACRED TRUST

The demands of leadership can get over your head in a hurry.
But there's one Person who's never overwhelmed.

THE WORD FOR THE DAY

DAVID MADE HIS MISTAKES, BUT HE WAS ALWAYS WILLING TO GET UP AND PUT HIS TRUST IN THE LORD . . . AGAIN.

———— ∞ ————

BE LISTENING FOR GOD'S WISDOM AT ANY HOUR OF THE DAY, FOR "EVEN AT NIGHT MY HEART INSTRUCTS ME."

———— ∞ ————

GOD IS NOT JUST A QUIET TIME COMPANION BUT THE "RIGHT HAND" MAN OF THE CHRISTIAN.

———— ∞ ————

JOB SECURITY? GOD'S PLAN FOR YOU IS MUCH MORE SECURE THAN THAT.

———— ∞ ————

TRUSTING GOD ALLOWS YOU TO SEE YOUR DAILY DECISIONS FROM AN ETERNAL PERSPECTIVE.

Psalm 16:1-2, 5-11

Keep me safe, O God, for in you I take refuge.

I said to the LORD, "You are my Lord; apart from you I have no good thing. . . ."

LORD, you have assigned me my portion and my cup; you have made my lot secure.

The boundary lines have fallen for me in pleasant places; surely I have a delightful inheritance.

I will praise the LORD, who counsels me; even at night my heart instructs me.

I have set the LORD always before me. Because he is at my right hand, I shall not be shaken.

Therefore my heart is glad and my tongue rejoices; my body also will rest secure, because you will not abandon me to the grave, nor will you let your Holy One see decay.

You have made known to me the path of life; you will fill me with joy in your presence, with eternal pleasures at your right hand.

THE VOICE OF WISDOM

Some years ago, I heard a speaker relate an old Egyptian saying: "The archer strikes the target partly by pulling, partly by letting go."

Our attitude will change when we let go. It can be difficult. We strain, pull, and struggle, trying to hold on. Our hopes and plans for the future result in frantic anxiety when our problems would be solved if we let go and gave God control.

Have you noticed that human efforts do not always achieve success? When we turn our anxieties over to God, His plans for us give the best direction for our lives. Our attitudes change when we accept God's superior plan. We are assured that miracles do happen when God takes charge.

This is most likely to happen when we pray for what God wants, not for our own desires. It happens when we ask God to use us for His purposes, not for our own successes. Paul says, "I have strength for all things in Christ Who empowers me–I am ready for anything and equal to anything through Him Who infuses inner strength into me" (Philippians 4:13, Amplified).

–EDNA EDWARDS

Leadership & Principle

NUMBER 36

SUCCESSFUL LEADERS ARE ABLE TO LEAN THE FULL WEIGHT OF THEIR RESPONSIBILITY ON GOD'S ABILITY.

When you want something to be handled right, you're always better off leaving it in God's hands than in yours.

THE ONE YOU LOVE

You have promised your best to your leadership responsibility.
But you have promised your life to your husband.

THE WORD FOR THE DAY

PEOPLE OBVIOUSLY PLACE THEIR CONFIDENCE IN YOU. BUT NO ONE'S PRAISE SHOULD BE AS SWEET IN YOUR EARS AS YOUR OWN HUSBAND'S.

———— ✦ ————

SEEKING IN ALL THINGS TO "BRING GOOD, NOT HARM" IS PERHAPS THE MOST DESCRIPTIVE DEFINITION OF TRUE LOVE.

———— ✦ ————

THE BEST MARRIAGE IS THE ONE WHERE HUSBAND AND WIFE ARE BOTH SERVING EACH OTHER.

———— ✦ ————

HOME AND FAMILY CAN BECOME THE FIRST THINGS TO FALL OFF YOUR PRIORITY LIST. BUT YOUR GREATEST REWARD IN LIFE WILL COME FROM WHAT YOU ACCOMPLISH THERE.

Proverbs 31:10-12, 23-26, 28-31

A wife of noble character who can find? She is worth far more than rubies.

Her husband has full confidence in her and lacks nothing of value. She brings him good, not harm, all the days of her life. . . .

Her husband is respected at the city gate, where he takes his seat among the elders of the land.

She makes linen garments and sells them, and supplies the merchants with sashes. She is clothed with strength and dignity; she can laugh at the days to come. She speaks with wisdom, and faithful instruction is on her tongue. . . .

Her children arise and call her blessed; her husband also, and he praises her: "Many women do noble things, but you surpass them all."

Charm is deceptive, and beauty is fleeting; but a woman who fears the LORD is to be praised.

Give her the reward she has earned, and let her works bring her praise at the city gate.

THE VOICE OF WISDOM

Catherine Booth, co-founder of the Salvation Army, was a remarkably sensitive person. And her discernment showed best in her relationship to William, her husband. In a letter written to him, she declared her intent that their home would always be a place sensitive to his needs and concerns:

"If you will seek home, love home, be happy at home, I will spend my energies in trying to make it a more than ordinary one. It shall, if my ability can do it, be a spot sunny and bright, pure and calm, refined and tender, a fit school in which to train immortal spirits for a holy and glorious heaven, a fit resting place for a spirit pressed and anxious about public duties. But oh, I know it is easy to talk. I feel how liable I am to fall short. But it is well to purpose right, to aim high, to hope much. Yes, we will make home to each other the brightest spot on earth. We will be tender, thoughtful, loving, and forbearing, will we not? Yes, we will."

These are the words of a woman who was reaching out to touch, who had looked within a man and found something to which she could minister.

–GAIL MACDONALD

Do something special for your husband today. It will remind him of your love, and remind you to love him.

WHO? ME?

*If you're feeling outmatched by a certain job or challenge,
you're probably right where God wants you to be.*

THE WORD FOR THE DAY

WHERE GOD GUIDES, GOD PROVIDES. MOSES, LIKE US, HAD ONLY ONE RESPONSIBILITY IN THIS SITUATION. TO OBEY.

GOD'S HEARD ALL YOUR EXCUSES BEFORE. IF HE HAS PLACED YOU IN A CERTAIN FIELD OF RESPONSIBILITY, HE WILL WORK THROUGH YOU.

UNSURE ABOUT WHETHER THIS TASK IS EVEN GOD'S WILL FOR YOU? STUDY THE WORD, SEEK WISE COUNSEL, AND TRUST GOD TO TURN EVEN YOUR MISTAKES INTO SUCCESSES.

"FOR WHEN I AM WEAK, THEN I AM STRONG" (2 CORINTHIANS 12:10).

Exodus 3:10-12a, 13, 4:1, 10-13

"I am sending you to Pharaoh to bring my people the Israelites out of Egypt."

But Moses said to God, "Who am I, that I should go to Pharaoh and bring the Israelites out of Egypt?" And God said, "I will be with you. . . ."

Moses said to God, "Suppose I go to the Israelites and say to them, 'The God of your fathers has sent me to you,' and they ask me, 'What is his name?' Then what shall I tell them? . . . What if they do not believe me or listen to me and say, 'The LORD did not appear to you'? . . . . O Lord, I have never been eloquent, neither in the past nor since you have spoken to your servant. I am slow of speech and tongue."

The LORD said to him, "Who gave man his mouth? Who makes him deaf or mute? Who gives him sight or makes him blind? Is it not I, the LORD?

"Now go; I will help you speak and will teach you what to say."

But Moses said, "O Lord, please send someone else to do it."

THE VOICE OF WISDOM

Lying paralyzed on a hospital bed, staring straight up at the ceiling, I seemed to hear the voice of God, saying, *Joni, I want you to live life without use of your hands or legs and learn to smile while doing it.*

What's more, God seemed to be saying, *I want you to be My audiovisual aid of how strength shows up best in weakness.*

"What? People won't believe in me. It'll be, 'How can God be good if He would allow something like permanent paralysis to happen to her? God must not be very caring or compassionate.'"

The fact was, I didn't believe in myself: "I can't do anything, not even peel an orange or walk across a room. What good am I to myself? To anybody?" Insecure and unsure, seething with doubts and resentments–that was me.

But I'm so grateful God reduced me to ashes in this wheelchair. In my weakness, I have learned, like Moses, to lean hard on God. The weaker I am, the harder I lean on Him. The harder I lean, the stronger I discover Him to be. The stronger I discover God to be, the more resolute I am in this job He's given me to do.

–JONI EARECKSON TADA

Insecurities are God's way of reminding you Who's in charge here. Trust His strength to keep you afloat.

GLORY TO GOD

Oh, the warm rush of pride when people pour on the praise.
But oh, how much sweeter, when it goes to God instead.

THE WORD FOR THE DAY

NEVER BELIEVE YOUR WORK IS AS GREAT AS PEOPLE SAY IT IS, NOR AS BAD AS PEOPLE SAY IT IS.

———— ❧ ————

SHOW THE DOOR TO EVERY PROUD THOUGHT THAT ENTERS YOUR HEAD. IT'S SATAN'S FAVORITE WAY IN. YOU'LL HAVE TO LEAN ON GOD HARD TO KEEP HIM OUT.

———— ❧ ————

SOMETIMES OUR SPIRITUAL WORDS JUST MAKE US LOOK MORE SPIRITUAL. IS GOD GETTING THE GLORY IN YOUR HEART?

———— ❧ ————

"NOT TO US, O LORD, NOT TO US BUT TO YOUR NAME BE THE GLORY, BECAUSE OF YOUR LOVE AND FAITHFULNESS" (PSALM 115:1).

Psalm 66:5, 8-12, 16-20

Come and see what God has done, how awesome his works on man's behalf....

Praise our God, O peoples, let the sound of his praise be heard; he has preserved our lives and kept our feet from slipping.

For you, O God, tested us; you refined us like silver. You brought us into prison and laid burdens on our backs.

You let men ride over our heads; we went through fire and water, but you brought us to a place of abundance....

Come and listen, all you who fear God; let me tell you what he has done for me.

I cried out to him with my mouth; his praise was on my tongue.

If I had cherished sin in my heart, the Lord would not have listened; but God has surely listened and heard my voice in prayer.

Praise be to God, who has not rejected my prayer or withheld his love from me!

THE VOICE OF WISDOM

A bright, searching young woman once asked me, "Was it not egotistical of God to create us for his glory?" This was an honest, legitimate question of one seeking to understand the purpose of her existence. She listened intently as I

Leadership Principle

NUMBER 39

GENUINE LEADERS GIVE GOD THE CREDIT FOR THEIR TALENTS AND SUCCESSES.

explained that it was not God's ego that caused him to create us for his glory. God is glorious in and of himself. He created us to reflect his glory because of *our* need, not *his* need. There is no other purpose that would have given us significance. Being created to reflect the glory of the Creator elevates us to a position of potential power in a way that nothing else could do.

When God's glory is our reason for being, we are freed from the entanglements of self-interest, self-promotion, and self-centeredness. We are freed from the domination of sin and liberated for our primary purpose. Freedom from the rule of sin releases the potential for which we were created–to reflect the glory of the Glorious One. Women reflect this glory by obeying the Master Designer's plan and offering all of their gifts to serve him.

–SUSAN HUNT

Your accolades are not yours to be taken personally, but are your own opportunities to give personal thanks to God.

REST FOR THE WEARY

*From one vantage point, rest can look like doing nothing.
But in reality, it's one of the most useful things you can do.*

THE WORD FOR THE DAY

GOD, OF COURSE, HAD NO NEED TO REST. "INDEED, HE WHO WATCHES OVER ISRAEL WILL NEITHER SLUMBER NOR SLEEP" (PSALM 121:4)

———

HIS RESTING WAS AN EXAMPLE TO US, WHICH HE LATER ISSUED AS COMMANDMENT #4, TEACHING US TO INCLUDE REST IN OUR ROUTINE.

———

"KEEPING IT HOLY" MEANS TO *SEPARATE* OR *SET APART* THE SABBATH FROM NORMAL EVERYDAY ACTIONS.

———

THE NEW TESTAMENT CALLS OUR SALVATION A "SABBATH-REST" FROM OUR LABORS (HEBREWS 4:10).

Genesis 1:31–2:2
Exodus 20:8–11

God saw all that he had made, and it was very good. And there was evening, and there was morning–the sixth day.

Thus the heavens and the earth were completed in all their vast array.

By the seventh day God had finished the work he had been doing; so on the seventh day he rested from all his work. . . .

"Remember the Sabbath day by keeping it holy. Six days you shall labor and do all your work, but the seventh day is a Sabbath to the LORD your God. On it you shall not do any work, neither you, nor your son or daughter, nor your manservant or maidservant, nor your animals, nor the alien within your gates.

"For in six days the LORD made the heavens and the earth, the sea, and all that is in them, but he rested on the seventh day. Therefore the LORD blessed the Sabbath day and made it holy."

THE VOICE OF WISDOM

Leadership Principle

NUMBER 40

MAKE YOURSELF TAKE TIME TO REST AND REFRESH.

The missionaries among whom I grew up were highly trained, thoroughly qualified, and deeply committed. They worked hard. At the same time, they knew that one essential part of hard work was recreation.

It is important that we take time out for ourselves–for relaxation, for refreshment. There have been times when I sat on the front porch, gently rocking and enjoying the view across the valley and the mountains beyond, yet I felt guilty because I wasn't doing something. Like a bow always strung tightly, we can lose our resilience. But I know the importance of releasing the string periodically to allow it to rest.

Elizabeth Goudge writes in her book, *A City of Bells*, "It is sometimes necessary in life to do nothing, but so few people do it nicely."

But while relaxation is one thing, refreshment is another. We need to drink frequently and at length from God's fresh springs, to spend time in the Scripture, time in fellowship with Him, time worshiping Him. Blaise Pascal wrote, "The sole cause of man's unhappiness is that he does not know how to stay quietly in his room."

–RUTH BELL GRAHAM

Life can keep your mind at work around the clock. You owe it to yourself to shut down for a little while.

YOUR RESPONSIBILITY

While others are blaming someone else or making excuses,
a quality leader is telling the accusers to start with her.

THE WORD FOR THE DAY

WHEN OTHERS POINT FINGERS AND QUESTION YOUR ABILITY, QUIETLY REMEMBER HOW LITTLE THEY KNOW ABOUT HOW MUCH YOU DO.

PAUL'S LEADERSHIP IN THE CHURCH CAUSED HIM TO BECOME "ITS SERVANT." YOUR LEADERSHIP WILL DO NO LESS.

YOUR RESPONSIBILITIES COULD KEEP YOU UP ALL NIGHT EVERY NIGHT IF YOU LET THEM. YOU MUST ALLOW GOD TO CARRY YOUR CONCERNS.

ASK GOD TO LET OTHERS SEE, NOT YOUR OWN CAPABILITIES, BUT "HIS ENERGY, WHICH SO POWERFULLY WORKS" IN YOU.

Colossians 1:24–2:1a

Now I rejoice in what was suffered for you, and I fill up in my flesh what is still lacking in regard to Christ's afflictions, for the sake of his body, which is the church.

I have become its servant by the commission God gave me to present to you the word of God in its fullness—the mystery that has been kept hidden for ages and generations, but is now disclosed to the saints.

To them God has chosen to make known among the Gentiles the glorious riches of this mystery, which is Christ in you, the hope of glory.

We proclaim him, admonishing and teaching everyone with all wisdom, so that we may present everyone perfect in Christ.

To this end I labor, struggling with all his energy, which so powerfully works in me.

I want you to know how much I am struggling for you. . . .

THE VOICE OF WISDOM

Leadership & Principle

NUMBER 41

LEADERS TAKE RESPONSIBILITY FOR WHAT HAPPENS UNDER THEIR WATCH.

While driving one day, I passed a worn-out farm. Deep gullies were cut through the fields where the dirt had been washed away by the rains. The creek had been allowed to change its course in the bottom of the field and had cut out a new channel, ruining the good land in its way. Tall weeds and brambles were taking strength from the soil.

Did you ever think how a bit of land shows the character of the owner? A dishonest greed is shown by robbing the soil. The traits of a spendthrift are shown in wasting the resources of the farm by destroying its woods and waters, while carelessness and laziness are seen in scars on the hillsides and washes in the lower fields.

It should be a matter of pride to keep our own farm, that little bit of the earth's surface for which we are responsible, in good condition, passing it on to our successor better than we found it. Trees should be growing where otherwise would be waste places, with the waters protected as much as possible from the hot sun and drying winds, with fields free from gullies and the soil fertile.

–LAURA INGALLS WILDER

Responsibility grows on you. As you practice it more faithfully today, you'll be even more ready for tomorrow.

I'M NOT SURPRISED

You'll meet lots of obstacles and opposition on the path of leadership.
But anything worth doing is worth fighting for.

THE WORD FOR THE DAY

SUCCESS IN A WORTHY
ENDEAVOR WILL STIR UP OPPO-
SITION. EFFECTIVE LEADERS
COUNTER WITH POSITIVE
WORDS AND PRODUCTIVE
ACTION.

——— ❧ ———

NEHEMIAH PRAYED TO GOD
AND POSTED A GUARD.
LEADERS PRAY, BUT LEADERS
ALSO ACT.

——— ❧ ———

REALISTIC PLANNING TAKES
ADVERSITY INTO ACCOUNT.

——— ❧ ———

CHALLENGES ARE MEANT TO BE
PREPARED FOR AND LEARNED
FROM, NOT TO BE AFRAID OF.

——— ❧ ———

WHEN PEOPLE ARE LED IN A
GREAT CAUSE, THEY WILL GO
TO GREAT LENGTHS TO SERVE.

Nehemiah 4:7-9, 13-15

But when Sanballat, Tobiah, the Arabs, the Ammonites and the men of Ashdod heard that the repairs to Jerusalem's walls had gone ahead and that the gaps were being closed, they were very angry.

They all plotted together to come and fight against Jerusalem and stir up trouble against it. But we prayed to our God and posted a guard day and night to meet this threat. . . .

Therefore I stationed some of the people behind the lowest points of the wall at the exposed places, posting them by families, with their swords, spears and bows.

After I looked things over, I stood up and said to the nobles, the officials and the rest of the people, "Don't be afraid of them. Remember the Lord, who is great and awesome, and fight for your brothers, your sons and your daughters, your wives and your homes."

When our enemies heard that we were aware of their plot and that God had frustrated it, we all returned to the wall, each to his own work.

THE VOICE OF WISDOM

Don't be surprised if there is an attack on your work, on you who are called to do it, on your innermost nature—the hidden person of the heart. It must be so. The great thing is not to be surprised, nor to count it strange—for that plays into the hand of the enemy.

Is it possible that anyone should set himself to exalt our beloved Lord and not instantly become a target for many arrows? Don't be surprised if you suffer. It is part of the way of the cross. Mark 9:12 says, "The Son of Man must suffer much." If we follow in the way He went, we also must suffer.

Have you ever gone through your Bible, marking the places where suffering in one form or another is mentioned? It's wonderfully enlightening. The Book is full of joy, but it is also full of pain, and pain is taken for granted. "Think it not strange. Count it all joy."

Oh, what a Book the Bible is! If only we steep our souls in its mighty comfort, we can't go far wrong, and we shall never lose heart.

So rejoice! You are giving Him what He asks you to give Him—the chance to show you what He can do.

—AMY CARMICHAEL

Leadership Principle

NUMBER 42

KNOW THAT OPPOSITION WILL CERTAINLY COME. BE READY FOR IT.

Listen and learn from the voice of challenge and opposition. But if you're sure you're doing right, press on through it.

A WORD OF THANKS

*When you say thanks to others, you build up a lot more
than their own esteem. You make yourself stand taller, too.*

THE WORD FOR THE DAY

PAUL SOMETIMES COMES OFF AS A LITTLE GRUFF, BUT HE LOVED THE PEOPLE IN THESE CHURCHES LIKE A FATHER.

❦

CAN YOU, LIKE PAUL, HONESTLY TELL THE PEOPLE YOU WORK AROUND THAT YOU'VE BEEN "MENTIONING [THEM] IN [YOUR] PRAYERS?"

❦

"YOU KNOW WE NEVER USED FLATTERY." IT'S BETTER TO SAY NOTHING THAN TO POUR ON THE PRAISE WITHOUT MEANING IT.

❦

GRATITUDE HAS BECOME A LOST VIRTUE IN OUR GENERATION. YOUR CHILDREN NEED TO SEE YOUR THANKFUL HEART.

1 Thessalonians
1:1-3, 2:5-8

Paul, Silas and Timothy, To the church of the Thessalonians in God the Father and the Lord Jesus Christ: Grace and peace to you.

We always thank God for all of you, mentioning you in our prayers.

We continually remember before our God and Father your work produced by faith, your labor prompted by love, and your endurance inspired by hope in our Lord Jesus Christ. . . .

You know we never used flattery, nor did we put on a mask to cover up greed—God is our witness.

We were not looking for praise from men, not from you or anyone else. As apostles of Christ we could have been a burden to you, but we were gentle among you, like a mother caring for her little children.

We loved you so much that we were delighted to share with you not only the gospel of God but our lives as well, because you had become so dear to us.

THE VOICE OF WISDOM

Thank you, God, for the people I work with. For their greeting in the morning and their good night when our work is done. For the sense of comradeship we have all day long. The happy ones and the cross ones, the sociable and the withdrawn.

Different though our natures, we meet for a common purpose, share common problems, and pursue common goals. The strange and wonderful bond of a job to be done together makes us kin.

We are not "one big happy family," yet a family, nonetheless. We rejoice like a family, squabble like a family, have little feuds and alliances like a family.

We try to help each other, are genuinely concerned about each other. There is an affection between us that only people who work together can understand.

And sometimes when the day is over and we are parting to go our separate ways, wonder fills me at all these people I have come to know and love through work. They have added something priceless to my life.

Bless and keep them always, these people I work with.

—MARJORIE HOLMES

Leadership & Principle

NUMBER 43

GOOD LEADERS REMEMBER WHAT THOSE WHO SERVE UNDER THEM HAVE DONE TO HELP.

Have you taken the time to say thanks to someone lately? Go out of your way to make it a top priority today.

ROUTINE SERVICE

*If the high road of leadership doesn't take you across
the low road of servanthood, you need to get some new directions.*

THE WORD FOR THE DAY

PERSONAL AMBITION ALWAYS
OBSCURES THE MAIN PURPOSE
OF THE GROUP OR ENDEAVOR.

———— ∽ ————

THE DISCIPLES GREW INDIG-
NANT, NOT OUT OF SHOCK AT
JAMES AND JOHN'S REQUEST,
BUT BECAUSE THEY SECRETLY
COVETED THE SAME THING FOR
THEMSELVES.
(SEE LUKE 24:22.)

———— ∽ ————

IF EVEN JESUS CAME TO EARTH
TO SERVE, YOU ARE HERE TO
SERVE, TOO.

———— ∽ ————

BUT IN YOUR ZEAL TO SERVE,
BE CAREFUL NOT TO WASTE
YOUR TIME DOING OTHERS'
WORK FOR THEM. YOU ARE
STILL RESPONSIBLE FOR CAST-
ING THE VISION.

Matthew 20:20-22, 24-28

Then the mother of Zebedee's sons came t
Jesus with her sons and, kneeling down, asked
favor of him.

"What is it you want?" he asked. She sai
"Grant that one of these two sons of mine may s
at your right and the other at your left in you
kingdom."

"You don't know what you are asking," Jesu
said to them. "Can you drink the cup I am goir
to drink?" "We can," they answered. . . .

When the ten heard about this, they were indi
nant with the two brothers.

Jesus called them together and said, "You kno
that the rulers of the Gentiles lord it over then
and their high officials exercise authority ov
them.

"Not so with you. Instead, whoever wants t
become great among you must be your servan
and whoever wants to be first must be your slave
just as the Son of Man did not come to be serve
but to serve, and to give his life as a ransom fo
many."

THE VOICE OF WISDOM

Why should you want to be a servant? Because, as the old saying goes, everything that goes around comes around. What you sow, you reap. These are not empty platitudes. If you want to influence others to serve and help you make a difference, you will get back what you give out. The service ethic always boomerangs.

Remember: People don't care how much you know until they know how much you care. They are not interested in your title, your college degrees, or how much money you have. First, they want to know if you care about them as a person, if you care about helping them solve their problem. Then your knowledge and experience becomes important.

When serving, ask yourself two questions. First, "What would I want if I were dealing with me?" That brings the idea of service to a very personal level. And second, "Who am I really serving?" If leadership serves only the leader, it will fail. Only when service for a common good is your primary purpose are you truly leading.

–SHEILA MURRAY BETHEL

Leadership
Principle

NUMBER 44

THE BEST LEADERS
ARE THE BEST
SERVANTS.

Consider how well you're serving those who serve you. And consider some ways you can even the balance.

GOD'S WORD ON IT

*Of all the great books out there on leadership styles
and people skills, only one can claim to have all your answers.*

WORLDLY WISDOM AND WAYS OF DOING THINGS CAN SOUND SO RIGHT SOMETIMES, BUT ONLY GOD'S WAY HAS THE RING OF TRUTH.

DON'T BE SPOOKED BY THE DISCIPLINE OF MEDITATION. DWELLING ON THE SCRIPTURE WILL CEMENT ITS TRUTHS IN YOUR LIFE.

STRIVE TO BE THE SAME IN BOTH "FRUIT" AND "LEAF"— IN BOTH THE PERSON YOU PROFESS TO BE AND THE PERSON YOU REALLY ARE.

THE BIBLE ISN'T TRUE BECAUSE IT WORKS. THE REASON IT WORKS IS BECAUSE IT'S TRUE.

Psalm 1:1-3
Psalm 19:7-11

Blessed is the man who does not walk in the counsel of the wicked or stand in the way of sinners or sit in the seat of mockers.

But his delight is in the law of the LORD, and on his law he meditates day and night.

He is like a tree planted by streams of water, which yields its fruit in season and whose leaf does not wither. Whatever he does prospers. . . .

The law of the LORD is perfect, reviving the soul. The statutes of the LORD are trustworthy, making wise the simple.

The precepts of the LORD are right, giving joy to the heart. The commands of the LORD are radiant, giving light to the eyes.

The fear of the LORD is pure, enduring forever. The ordinances of the LORD are sure and altogether righteous.

They are more precious than gold, than much pure gold; they are sweeter than honey, than honey from the comb.

By them is your servant warned; in keeping them there is great reward.

THE VOICE OF WISDOM

These words are for us. We may take them though they were spoken to another people in another age. All the green fields of the Scriptures are for all the sheep of His pasture. None are fenced off from us. Our Lord and Savior, the great Shepherd of the sheep Himself, led the way into these fields, as a study of His use of the Old Testament shows. His servants, the writers of the New Testament, followed Him there. And so may we. The words of the Lord are as much for us as for His ancient people Israel.

Hammer this truth out on the anvil of experience–this truth that the loving thoughts of God direct and perfect all that concerns us. It will bear to be beaten out to the uttermost. The pledged word of God to man is no puffball to break at a touch and scatter into dust. It is iron. It is gold, the most malleable of metals. It is more golden than gold. It abides imperishable for-ever.

I have been told, "It is possible to gather gold, where it may be had, with moonlight." By moonlight, then, let us gather our gold.

–AMY CARMICHAEL

You can tell how seriously you're seeking the will of God by checking how much time you're seeking it in His Word.

SAY WHAT?

People listen to what you have to say. But sometimes the things you don't say are the most eloquent words of all.

THE WORD FOR THE DAY

JESUS WASN'T DODGING ANY-
THING HERE. HE JUST WASN'T
GIVING THEM THE SATISFACTION
OF SEEING HIM CRACK.

━━━ ❧ ━━━

WHEN YOU FEEL ANGER BURN-
ING YOUR NECK, THAT'S WHEN
YOU'LL KNOW WHETHER YOU
HAVE YOUR TONGUE
UNDER CONTROL.

━━━ ❧ ━━━

JESUS WAS THE MASTER AT
USING THE RIGHT WORDS. HE
WASN'T AFRAID TO OFFEND IN
ORDER TO MAKE PEOPLE
SQUIRM AT THEIR OWN
INDIFFERENCE.

━━━ ❧ ━━━

"A GENTLE ANSWER TURNS
AWAY WRATH, BUT A HARSH
WORD STIRS UP ANGER"

(PROVERBS 15:1).

Mark 14:53, 60-62a
Mark 15:1-5

They took Jesus to the high priest, and all the chief priests, elders and teachers of the law came together....

Then the high priest stood up before them and asked Jesus, "Are you not going to answer? What is this testimony that these men are bringing against you?"

But Jesus remained silent and gave no answer. Again the high priest asked him, "Are you the Christ, the Son of the Blessed One?"

"I am," said Jesus....

Very early in the morning, the chief priests, with the elders, the teachers of the law and the whole Sanhedrin, reached a decision. They bound Jesus, led him away and turned him over to Pilate.

"Are you the king of the Jews?" asked Pilate.
"Yes, it is as you say," Jesus replied.

The chief priests accused him of many things. So again Pilate asked him, "Aren't you going to answer? See how many things they are accusing you of."

But Jesus still made no reply, and Pilate was amazed.

THE VOICE OF WISDOM

Groups are made up of all sorts of people who have very different personality types. We can avoid possible conflicts when we understand why people act and react as they do. By knowing others' strengths and weaknesses, we

can better encourage and build them up, thus fulfilling our leadership role.

I will never forget leaving a Christmas Missionary Dinner with the chairperson. The event went very well indeed, but in my choleric mode (can't relax, little tolerance for mistakes, and can do everything better), I proceeded to tell her how I thought we could improve the event the next year. Big mistake!

There is danger in becoming more interested in the subject, program, or event than in people. Don't lose the personal touch. I violated this principle. Virginia, who is deep and thoughtful, was quick to point out, "Judy, I would like to reflect on today and enjoy it. Could we talk about this later?"

That hurt. And it was a hard lesson for me. But now I am more observant and discerning before speaking my mind.

–JUDY HAMLIN

Maybe you've already blown it in the last 24 hours. Maybe the next thing you need to say to someone is an apology.

IT'S FAMILY TIME

The best way to overcome the guilt of seeing your leadership role cost your family is to not make it cost them anymore.

THE WORD FOR THE DAY

YOUR CHILDREN WILL ONLY BE YOUNG ONCE. THINK TWICE BEFORE YOU TAKE EXTRA TIME AWAY FROM THEM.

WATCH FOR AS-YOU-GO OPPORTUNITIES TO TEACH SPIRITUAL LESSONS TO YOUR CHILDREN WITHIN THE FLOW OF LIFE. SO YOU DON'T FORGET, KEEP A NOTEPAD WITH YOU TO JOT DOWN THINGS YOU WANT TO REMEMBER TO TELL YOUR KIDS.

TRY TO INVOLVE YOUR FAMILY AS MUCH AS POSSIBLE IN YOUR WORK.

GUARD AGAINST THE UNCHECKED WORDS OF WEARINESS AND FATIGUE.

Deuteronomy 6:4-9
Proverbs 6:20-23

Hear, O Israel: The LORD our God, the LORD is one. Love the LORD your God with all your heart and with all your soul and with all your strength.

These commandments that I give you today are to be upon your hearts.

Impress them on your children. Talk about them when you sit at home and when you walk along the road, when you lie down and when you get up.

Tie them as symbols on your hands and bind them on your foreheads. Write them on the doorframes of your houses and on your gates. . . .

My son, keep your father's commands and do not forsake your mother's teaching. Bind them upon your heart forever; fasten them around your neck.

When you walk, they will guide you; when you sleep, they will watch over you; when you awake, they will speak to you.

For these commands are a lamp, this teaching is a light, and the corrections of discipline are the way to life.

THE VOICE OF WISDOM

The affluence enjoyed by this generation has been both curse and blessing. We are blessed beyond imagination, being able to provide for our children unprecedented opportunities. On the other hand, we have in some ways been cursed with the mobility and mechanization which has often cut into our family time.

There is no greater need in Christian homes than that time be faithfully allotted and earnestly guarded for the family to be alone in worship and praise to the Creator and in fun and fellowship with one another. God has never wavered from His plan to use the family unit in teaching spiritual truth, in undergirding the work of the kingdom, and in ministering to one another in love.

Are your spouse and children important enough to you to schedule regular, uninterrupted times to be with them–and to focus upon them with the same commitment you would have in preparing a meal, cleaning a room, or pursuing a career goal?

May God give us Christian homes alive with laughter and fun and secure in relaxation and contentment!

–DOROTHY KELLEY PATTERSON

Nothing wrong with being spontaneous, but what's something you can go ahead and plan to do together as a family?

ON LOAN FROM GOD

Your leadership gift doesn't make you better than anyone else.
But it does make you responsible for investing it well.

THE WORD FOR THE DAY

PLAYING DOWN YOUR LEADERSHIP GIFT MAY HELP YOU FEEL HUMBLE, BUT IT TELLS GOD YOU'RE NOT HAPPY WITH WHAT HE GAVE YOU.

———— ❧ ————

THE REASON GOD GAVE YOU YOUR SPECIFIC SKILLS IS "SO THAT THE BODY OF CHRIST MAY BE BUILT UP."

———— ❧ ————

A CHURCH WHERE THE MEMBERS KNOW THEIR SPIRITUAL GIFTS AND ARE EXERCISING THEM CONSISTENTLY IS A CHURCH THAT IS OPERATING THE WAY GOD INTENDED.

———— ❧ ————

EMBRACE YOUR CALLING AS YOUR "REASONABLE SERVICE" (ROMANS 12:1)

Ephesians 4:7, 11–16

But to each one of us grace has been given as Christ apportioned it. . . .

It was he who gave some to be apostles, some to be prophets, some to be evangelists, and some to be pastors and teachers, to prepare God's people for works of service, so that the body of Christ may be built up until we all reach unity in the faith and in the knowledge of the Son of God and become mature, attaining to the whole measure of the fullness of Christ.

Then we will no longer be infants, tossed back and forth by the waves, and blown here and there by every wind of teaching and by the cunning and craftiness of men in their deceitful scheming.

Instead, speaking the truth in love, we will in all things grow up into him who is the Head, that is, Christ.

From him the whole body, joined and held together by every supporting ligament, grows and builds itself up in love, as each part does its work.

THE VOICE OF WISDOM

If you find yourself in the working world, for whatever reason, and you are not motivated to go to greater heights in your career, ask yourself if you are using the talents given you to their fullest. Could it be laziness that is keeping you from pushing ahead? Are you squandering abilities that could be used? Remember, God expects us to do our work with the highest possible excellence.

On the other hand, you may have ambitions that are not related to the working world. Your talents and ambitions may be more geared to other types of service. If you are using your talent as God would have it used, whether it furthers your career or not, then you are being a good and faithful servant.

So is it all right not to be ambitious for promotions and titles and places of prominence in the working world? Absolutely. As long as you are certain that you are using your talents to your greatest ability and not hiding them. And as long as you continually bring your priorities before God and keep them in line with his purposes for your life.

–MARY WHELCHEL

Leadership Principle

NUMBER 48

LEADERSHIP IS A NOBLE SPIRITUAL GIFT TO BE HONORED AND HIGHLY ESTEEMED.

Thank God today for the privilege of being a leader–not to make you proud of yourself, but to give praise to Him.

OFF CENTER

*If you try to do everything that everyone expects of you,
you'll end up not doing the things that are most important.*

JESUS KNEW THE PEOPLE WANTED . . . MORE! MORE! THAT IS ALWAYS THE CALL OF THE CROWD.

———— ⟨⟩ ————

EVEN JESUS—WHO ACTUALLY DID CARRY THE WEIGHT OF THE WORLD ON HIS SHOULDERS— KNEW HOW TO SAY NO TO UNWISE DEMANDS.

———— ⟨⟩ ————

WOULD YOU BE ABLE TO SPOT THE LINE IN YOUR OWN LIFE WHERE RESPONSIBILITY SLIPS OVER INTO EGO?

———— ⟨⟩ ————

DELEGATE. THEY MAY NOT DO IT JUST THE WAY YOU WOULD. (NO, THEY MIGHT BE ABLE TO DO IT BETTER.)

Luke 4:23-30

Jesus said to them, "Surely you will quote this proverb to me: 'Physician, heal yourself! Do here in your home town what we have heard that you did in Capernaum.' I tell you the truth," he continued, "no prophet is accepted in his hometown.

"I assure you that there were many widows in Israel in Elijah's time, when the sky was shut for three and a half years and there was a severe famine throughout the land. Yet Elijah was not sent to any of them, but to a widow in Zarephath in the region of Sidon.

"And there were many in Israel with leprosy in the time of Elisha the prophet, yet not one of them was cleansed–only Naaman the Syrian."

All the people in the synagogue were furious when they heard this. They got up, drove him out of the town, and took him to the brow of the hill on which the town was built, in order to throw him down the cliff.

But he walked right through the crowd and went on his way.

THE VOICE OF WISDOM

LEADERS CANNOT LET THEIR SCHEDULE BE DETERMINED BY DISTRACTIONS.

Urgency becomes a habit, and habits, as we all know, are hard to break. Sometimes it's easier to say "yes" to the one extra thing that will ruin the peace of our day because we have not sufficiently developed the ability to say "no." Sometimes the habit of riding the whitewater of urgency is easier than struggling against the current.

Human beings tend to do exactly what we want to do, despite our protestations to the contrary. When I'm tempted to let myself get caught up in a net of urgency, I need to look closely to see what I am getting as a reward. Do I really want peace? Do I really want the self-examination that time alone with God allows? Am I willing to let chores and errands slide so that I can experience a less hectic day? When night comes, which is more important: to feel my own personal accomplishment, or God's tranquillity?

As the days slide into years, and years into lifetimes, we wonder: Will we find ourselves with unfinished lists left by the bedside, or will we find ourselves at peace? A frightening question, but one worth asking.

–LESLIE WILLIAMS

You'll be asked to do more than you can get done today. Decide ahead of time how you'll deal with distractions.

WATCHING YOUR BACK

Often as a leader, you have to trust your own judgment.
But do you have someone to help you keep it trustworthy?

THE WORD FOR THE DAY

KING SAUL ONCE RECEIVED A SIMILAR REBUKE, BUT RESPONDED WITH GASPS AND EXCUSES INSTEAD OF DAVID'S HUMBLE APOLOGIES.

———— ❧ ————

THE LORD MET DAVID AND RESTORED HIM. IF GOD CAN GIVE A SECOND CHANCE, SHOULDN'T YOU?

———— ❧ ————

DAVID STILL PAID DEARLY FOR HIS INDISCRETIONS. DON'T THINK "I'M SORRY" MAKES EVERYTHING GO AWAY.

———— ❧ ————

RETURN THE FAVOR. OFFER YOURSELF AS AN ACCOUNTABILITY PARTNER TO A FRIEND OR FELLOW CHRISTIAN LEADER.

2 Samuel 12:1-4, 7, 9, 13

The LORD sent Nathan to David. When he came to him, he said, "There were two men in a certain town, one rich and the other poor. The rich man had a very large number of sheep and cattle, but the poor man had nothing except one little ewe lamb that he had bought.

"He raised it, and it grew up with him and his children. It shared his food, drank from his cup and even slept in his arms. It was like a daughter to him.

"Now a traveler came to the rich man, but the rich man refrained from taking one of his own sheep or cattle to prepare a meal for the traveler who had come to him. Instead, he took the ewe lamb that belonged to the poor man and prepared it for the one who had come to him. . . ."

Then Nathan said to David, "You are the man! . . . Why did you despise the word of the LORD by doing what is evil in his eyes? You did it in secret, but I will do this thing in broad daylight before all Israel." Then David said to Nathan, "I have sinned against the LORD."

THE VOICE OF WISDOM

One day when I was in the midst of finishing up the final manuscript on the book, *Smart Women Keep It Simple*, the children came home from school. I met them at the door and said, "I have to get this book done today. There will be no supper tonight. Don't talk to me. Don't ask me any questions. You'll just have to do the best you can."

Nathan, my perceptive and disgustingly honest teenaged son, said, "Mom, what's the name of that book you're working on?" I sheepishly confessed that the book was about making our lives simple and in balance with godly priorities. He then went on to console my punctured heart by saying, "Mom, you're really not a hypocrite, because before you started the book, you really did have your priorities straight."

What would I do without my family to keep me honest? I pity those public people who don't have the advantage of brutally honest friends and family to pull them back and challenge them to line up their lives with the message they speak. There is nothing more tragic than to be a public success and a private failure.

—ANNIE CHAPMAN

Leadership Principle

NUMBER 50

WISE LEADERS MAKE THEMSELVES ACCOUNTABLE TO SOMEONE ELSE.

How much better to heed a warning than to suffer the consequences. Have you activated your own security system?

TOTAL STEWARDSHIP

The way we talk about stewardship, you'd think money was all we cared about. But God cares about a lot more than that.

THE WORD FOR THE DAY

EVERYTHING WE HAVE BELONGS TO GOD. THAT ONE TRUTH SHOULD FOREVER CHANGE THE WAY WE VIEW THE THINGS AROUND US.

LYDIA OPENED HER HOME TO OUTSIDERS. IS YOUR DOOR OPEN TO ANYONE WHO NEEDS WHAT YOU CAN GIVE?

IF YOU HAVE MANAGEMENT OVER OTHERS' RESOURCES, ALWAYS BE SURE YOU TREAT THEM AS IF THEY WERE YOUR OWN.

YOUR FAITHFULNESS IN DAILY THINGS CREATES AN "OBEDI-ENCE THAT ACCOMPANIES YOUR CONFESSION." GOOD STEWARDSHIP MAKES YOU A WHOLE PERSON.

Acts 16:13-15
2 Corinthians 9:13-14

On the Sabbath we went outside the city gate to the river, where we expected to find a place of prayer. We sat down and began to speak to the women who had gathered there.

One of those listening was a woman named Lydia, a dealer in purple cloth from the city of Thyatira, who was a worshiper of God. The Lord opened her heart to respond to Paul's message.

When she and the members of her household were baptized, she invited us to her home. "If you consider me a believer in the Lord," she said, "come and stay at my house." And she persuaded us. . . .

Because of the service by which you have proved yourselves, men will praise God for the obedience that accompanies your confession of the gospel of Christ, and for your generosity in sharing with them and with everyone else.

And in their prayers for you their hearts will go out to you, because of the surpassing grace God has given you.

THE VOICE OF WISDOM

Being a Christian was a very practical matter for Lydia. She did not become a nun, nor even a full-time evangelist. She remained in her occupation. She brought credit to her name by submitting herself, her business, and her possessions to maximum service for Christ.

From then on, Lydia's earnings would not be an end in themselves, but a means to further the gospel. Lydia would sell purple to the honor of God.

The news spread quickly from her commercial city situated on several international trade routes. From then on, not only would bags of purple leave Lydia's home, but the gospel too would travel throughout the civilized world. It is reasonable to assume that a woman who could impress the apostles and her household with her newly found convictions would be no less successful in convincing her business contacts. Thus, her business was a two-fold success.

Lydia had been given much and she used it for the Lord. She is touching proof of how much God can do through a person who has made Him the first priority in life.

–GIEN KARSSEN

Leadership Principle

NUMBER 51

THE BEST LEADERS KNOW HOW TO BE GOOD STEWARDS OF ALL THEIR RESOURCES.

You have a lot more than money in your pocket of blessings. Are you willing to turn them inside out for His glory?

OPPORTUNITY CALLS

*The greatest victories you will win as a leader will be
the ones that seemed the most unwinnable at the start.*

THE WORD FOR THE DAY

"BE STRONG AND COURA-
GEOUS." THERE IS NO SUBSTI-
TUTE FOR BOLDNESS AND NO
VICTORY WITHOUT A FIGHT.

―――――

MOSES' DEATH LEFT JOSHUA
WITH SOME BIG SHOES TO FILL.
DO YOU SOMETIMES FEEL LIKE
YOU'RE IN OVER YOUR HEAD?
RELAX. YOU'RE IN
GOOD COMPANY.

―――――

GOD TOLD JOSHUA TO REFER
TO HIS WORD FOR GUIDANCE.
THE BIBLE IS FULL OF
PROMISES. READ THEM.
BELIEVE THEM.

―――――

MAKE THOUGHTFUL PLANS TO
MOVE AHEAD WITH YOUR
ESTABLISHED OBJECTIVES, THEN
PROCEED WITH
PRAYER AND ACTION.

Joshua 1:6-11a, 16

"Be strong and courageous, because you will
lead these people to inherit the land I swore to
their forefathers to give them.

"Be strong and very courageous. Be careful to
obey all the law my servant Moses gave you; do
not turn from it to the right or to the left, that you
may be successful wherever you go.

"Do not let this Book of the Law depart from
your mouth; meditate on it day and night, so that
you may be careful to do everything written in it.
Then you will be prosperous and successful.

"Have I not commanded you? Be strong and
courageous. Do not be terrified; do not be discouraged, for the LORD your God will be with you
wherever you go."

So Joshua ordered the officers of the people: "Go
through the camp and tell the people, 'Get your
supplies ready. Three days from now you will
cross the Jordan. . . .'"

Then they answered Joshua, "Whatever you
have commanded us we will do, and wherever
you send us we will go.

THE VOICE OF WISDOM

Now Moses was dead. Joshua, Moses' servant, was in charge as God's appointed successor. Until now, Joshua had been at Moses' side and had always had Moses to depend upon.

Leadership Principle

NUMBER 52

LEADERS SEE CHALLENGES AS OPPORTUNITIES.

Now he stood alone with the people facing a flooding Jordan River. Across that river was the land of Canaan, the country God had promised to Abraham, Isaac, and Jacob. It had been forty years since Joshua spied out this well-fortified land filled with giants. And those same Hittites, Jebusites, Amalekites, and all the other "ites" who had intimidated the Israelites forty years earlier were still there!

Can you imagine being in Joshua's sandals, having not only to take over for Moses but also to face such enemies? We don't know whether Joshua's knees were knocking, but we do know God had much to say to him about courage.

It was courage rather than discouragement that would bring the children of Israel into the promises of God. And courage rather than discouragement will also bring you and me into the promises of God.

–KAY ARTHUR

Try not to concentrate so much on the obstacles that lie ahead as on the reward that's waiting just beyond them.

OUT IN THE OPEN

*Some people seem to look for conflict, others to avoid it.
Smart leaders know when to let it go and when to air it out.*

THE WORD FOR THE DAY

PAUL OPPOSED PETER "TO HIS FACE." THAT'S ALWAYS BETTER THAN OPPOSING SOMEONE BEHIND THEIR BACK.

⸺ ⸙ ⸺

PETER HAD THE INFLUENCE TO SET POLICY AND PRECEDENT IN THE EARLY CHURCH. AND PAUL HAD THE COURAGE TO FORCE HIM TO RECONSIDER HIS POSITION.

⸺ ⸙ ⸺

"EVEN BARNABAS WAS LED ASTRAY." IF IMPORTANT ISSUES ARE LEFT UNRESOLVED, GOOD PEOPLE GET HURT BAD.

⸺ ⸙ ⸺

LEADERS CAN'T LET EVEN THE FAMILIAR TUG OF FRIENDSHIP KEEP THEM FROM POINTING OUT GLARING ERRORS.

Galatians 2:11-14, 19-20

When Peter came to Antioch, I opposed him to his face, because he was clearly in the wrong.

Before certain men came from James, he used to eat with the Gentiles. But when they arrived, he began to draw back and separate himself from the Gentiles because he was afraid of those who belonged to the circumcision group.

The other Jews joined him in his hypocrisy, so that by their hypocrisy even Barnabas was led astray.

When I saw that they were not acting in line with the truth of the gospel, I said to Peter in front of them all, "You are a Jew, yet you live like a Gentile and not like a Jew. How is it, then, that you force Gentiles to follow Jewish customs?" . . .

For through the law I died to the law so that I might live for God.

I have been crucified with Christ and I no longer live, but Christ lives in me. The life I live in the body, I live by faith in the Son of God, who loved me and gave himself for me.

THE VOICE OF WISDOM

Controversy is often necessary if people are to feel committed to decisions. When a thorough discussion is used to air different opinions and ideas, people are likely to feel satisfied and believe they have benefited from the discussion. They enjoy the excitement, feel aroused by the challenges of the conflict, and usually develop positive attitudes. They are committed to new agreements or positions because they understand how these new agreements are related to their own interests and positions. When the position is different from their own, they better understand why the adopted position is superior to their original one.

As a result of discussions about conflict, people disclose previously hidden information, challenge their own and others' assumptions, dig into issues, and as a consequence, understand the problem more thoroughly. In most cases, this results in more successful decisions.

The diverse opinions that create conflict are needed to help us better solve problems. In this way, conflict becomes the medium by which problems are recognized and solved.

–SHIRLEY SCHOOLEY

The first step toward defending the things you care about is to care about things that are worth defending.

SHARING THE LOAD

*Every time you hand off some task or assignment,
you're making an investment in someone else, as well as in yourself.*

THE WORD FOR THE DAY

YOU THINK *YOUR* JOB IS
TOUGH. MOSES HAD
ASSUMED TOTAL
RESPONSIBILITY FOR JUDGING
THE DISPUTES OF MORE THAN
3 MILLION PEOPLE.

JETHRO REPRIMANDED MOSES
FOR HIS POOR MANAGEMENT.
ALWAYS BE WILLING TO ACCEPT
SOUND ADVICE—EVEN FROM
YOUR IN-LAWS!

MOSES WAS TOLD TO "SELECT
CAPABLE MEN." NOT JUST
ANYONE WILL DO
WHEN YOU DELEGATE.

MOSES GAVE SOME OF HIS
SUBORDINATES MORE JURISDIC-
TION THAN OTHERS. ASSIGN
PEOPLE TASKS THAT ARE EQUAL
TO THEIR CAPABILITIES.

Exodus 18:14-15, 17, 19, 21-22

When his father-in-law saw all that Moses was doing for the people, he said, "What is this you are doing for the people? Why do you alone sit as judge, while all these people stand round you from morning till evening?"

Moses answered him, "Because the people come to me to seek God's will. ..."

Moses' father-in-law replied, ... "Listen now to me and I will give you some advice, and may God be with you. You must be the people's representative before God and bring their disputes to him...

"But select capable men from all the people— men who fear God, trustworthy men who hate dishonest gain—and appoint them as officials over thousands, hundreds, fifties and tens.

"Have them serve as judges for the people at all times, but have them bring every difficult case to you; the simple cases they can decide themselves. That will make your load lighter, because they will share it with you."

THE VOICE OF WISDOM

According to Everett T. Suters, author of *Succeed in Spite of Yourself*, senior management does not look favorably on the manager who has become irreplaceable. Irreplaceable managers have become logams holding up decisions, activities, and the growth of other employees.

That thought often runs contrary to some managers' thinking because many have the wrong concept of delegation. They look on delegation as dumping the undesirable tasks on their employees or as shirking their own responsibilities when they don't have time to get them done. Neither is the case.

Delegation, just as in Moses' day, is a means for developing others to their fullest potential in a way that will help everyone reach the desired goal.

Jesus spent three years preparing His disciples to carry on the ministry that has been growing for the last two thousand years in His earthly absence. Have you spent comparable time in developing your own employees who look to you for leadership?

Irreplaceable is not a compliment. It's a trap.

–DIANNA BOOHER

What are the top three items on your to-do list that never get done? Could someone else do what you can't get to?

HONESTLY

You're not a bald-faced liar. But has it become easy to tell less than you know, to cloak the truth in prettier clothes?

THE WORD FOR THE DAY

YOU'LL BE GLAD YOU WERE UP-FRONT WITH PEOPLE TODAY INSTEAD OF HAVING TO COVER YOUR OWN TRACKS TOMORROW.

HONESTY IS ABOUT MUCH MORE THAN YOUR WORDS. HONESTY IS A WAY OF LIFE, A LOOK ON YOUR FACE, A PURITY IN ALL YOUR MOTIVES.

THERE IS NO SUBSTITUTE FOR "A CLEAR CONSCIENCE." YOU CAN WITHSTAND A LOT OF HEAT WHEN YOUR OWN HEART CAN DEFEND YOU.

"LIVE PEACEFUL AND QUIET LIVES IN ALL GODLINESS AND HOLINESS" (1 TIMOTHY 2:2).

Hebrews 13:15-21

Through Jesus, therefore, let us continually offer to God a sacrifice of praise–the fruit of lips that confess his name. And do not forget to do good and to share with others, for with such sacrifices God is pleased.

Obey your leaders and submit to their authority. They keep watch over you as men who must give an account. Obey them so that their work will be a joy, not a burden, for that would be of no advantage to you.

Pray for us. We are sure that we have a clear conscience and desire to live honorably in every way. I particularly urge you to pray so that I may be restored to you soon.

May the God of peace, who through the blood of the eternal covenant brought back from the dead our Lord Jesus, that great Shepherd of the sheep, equip you with everything good for doing his will, and may he work in us what is pleasing to him, through Jesus Christ, to whom be glory for ever and ever. Amen.

THE VOICE OF WISDOM

Leadership & Principle

NUMBER 55

**ALWAYS
BE
HONEST.**

Is it possible that honesty is "the best policy" after all, actually and literally?

To do the right thing is simply to be honest, for being honest is more than refraining from short-changing a customer or robbing a neighbor's hen roost. To be sure, those items are included, but there is more to honesty than that. There is such a thing as being dishonest when no question of financial gain or loss is involved. When one person robs another of his good name, he is dishonest. When by an unnecessary, unkind act or cross word, one causes another to lose a day or an hour of happiness, is that one not a thief? Many a person robs another of the joy of life while taking pride in his own integrity. We are not honest even with ourselves.

If there were a cry of "Stop thief!" we would all stand still. Yet nevertheless in spite of our carelessness, we all know deep in our hearts that it pays to do the right thing, though it is easy to deceive ourselves for a time. If we do the wrong thing, we are quite likely never to know what we have lost by it.

–LAURA INGALLS WILDER

Make up your mind that you will always face every question honestly, every problem squarely, every person openly.

ONE DAY, ONE STEP

*God's timeframe can seem very slow to this world's way of thinking.
But who do you think knows the best way?*

THE WORD FOR THE DAY

ABRAHAM AND SARAH GOT IMPATIENT AND SOUGHT A MORE LOGICAL WAY TO GOD'S WILL. TRUST HIM TO MAKE GOOD ON HIS PROMISES, BUT IN HIS OWN TIME.

———

THEIR PLAN SEEMED FOOL-PROOF, BUT RESULTED IN ANGER, DISCORD, AND PERMANENT DAMAGE TO THEIR FAMILY.

———

ACTIONS HAVE CONSEQUENCES, NOT ONLY FOR THE SHORT RUN, BUT EVEN MORE DRAMATICALLY FOR THE LONG TERM.

———

SHORT CUTS WILL RARELY TAKE YOU TO YOUR DESIRED DESTINATION, AND NEVER IN THE WAY GOD INTENDED.

Genesis 16:1-6

Now Sarai, Abram's wife, had borne him no children. But she had an Egyptian maidservant named Hagar; so she said to Abram, "The LORD has kept me from having children. Go, sleep with my maidservant; perhaps I can build a family through her." Abram agreed to what Sarai said.

So after Abram had been living in Canaan ten years, Sarai his wife took her Egyptian maidservant Hagar and gave her to her husband to be his wife.

He slept with Hagar, and she conceived. When she knew she was pregnant, she began to despise her mistress.

Then Sarai said to Abram, "You are responsible for the wrong I am suffering. I put my servant in your arms, and now that she knows she is pregnant, she despises me. May the LORD judge between you and me."

"Your servant is in your hands," Abram said. "Do with her whatever you think best." Then Sarai mistreated Hagar; so she fled from her.

Even Jesus, clear as he was about his calling, had to get his instructions one day at a time. One time he was told to wait, another time to go.

One of my business advisors told me about a friend of his who is now living his dream: owning and running a resort hotel in Hawaii. "Do you know how he got there?" he asked. "By flipping pancakes . . . one flip at a time." This man's dream was to own a hotel, but he didn't have any money. So he signed on as a cook at a pancake house and was soon promoted to manager. Then he and the owner teamed up and bought another pancake house and another. It wasn't long before their little pancake house real estate empire had been sold and turned into a resort hotel in Hawaii. He started out as a cook and took one step at a time.

And so when I would come to Ron full of eagerness and frustration about what my next step could be, asking a thousand questions about how I was going to get there, he would smile at me and say, "Flip . . . flip . . . flip," making little pancake motions with his hands.

Jesus took one step at a time.

–LAURIE BETH JONES

Leadership Principle

NUMBER 56

THE END NEVER JUSTIFIES THE MEANS. WE MUST TRY TO ADHERE TO GOD'S TIMING.

Is God's plan taking longer to develop than you thought? Wait him out anyway. You'll never think of a better one.

OPEN TO ANYTHING

The world in which you lead can be all-consuming at times, but serving in God's Kingdom is all-important all the time.

THE WORD FOR THE DAY

PAUL WANTED TO TAKE THE GOSPEL NORTH, BUT WHEN THE SPIRIT LED HIM WEST, HE FOLLOWED WILLINGLY.

———— ❧ ————

IT DOESN'T SAY HOW THE SPIRIT PREVENTED THEM. BUT IT'S CLEAR THAT GOD HAS WAYS OF MAKING HIS DIRECTION KNOWN.

———— ❧ ————

DECISIONS THAT ARE SEEMINGLY SMALL CAN HAVE AN ENORMOUS IMPACT ON THE FUTURE.

———— ❧ ————

PAUL WAS JOINED IN HIS EFFORTS BY A NUMBER OF COMPANIONS. DO YOU HAVE FRIENDS ALONGSIDE TO HELP YOU RECOGNIZE GOD'S COURSE OF ACTION?

Acts 16:6-10, 13-14

Paul and his companions traveled throughout the region of Phrygia and Galatia, having been kept by the Holy Spirit from preaching the word in the province of Asia.

When they came to the border of Mysia, they tried to enter Bithynia, but the Spirit of Jesus would not allow them to. So they passed by Mysia and went down to Troas.

During the night Paul had a vision of a man of Macedonia standing and begging him, "Come over to Macedonia and help us." After Paul had seen the vision, we got ready at once to leave for Macedonia, concluding that God had called us to preach the gospel to them. . . .

On the Sabbath we went outside the city gate to the river, where we expected to find a place of prayer. We sat down and began to speak to the women who had gathered there.

One of those listening was a woman named Lydia, a dealer in purple cloth from the city of Thyatira, who was a worshiper of God. The Lord opened her heart to respond to Paul's message.

God often rewrites daily planners. When He does so, He's saying, "This is what I want you to do today."

Then once we submit to His control, we're free to approach each day with a positive attitude: "Lord, I've arranged my schedule to please You. But if You want to rearrange it, that's fine. Just don't let me waste my interruptions or disregard the significance of the changes You make. Rather, let me seize each challenge as Your opportunity."

After commitment comes implementation, which is always the hard part. Let's say the phone rings. We pick it up. As we do, we pray, "Lord, I need wisdom, love, and tact. Could You please give it now–and in abundance?"

A knock comes at the door. We open it. As we give the greeting, we're asking, "Lord, give me Your grace in manner and speech."

There is an unexpected, tense summons to the hospital. We go. On the way we admit, "I don't know what I'm going to see when I get there or how I'm going to react. Just make me Your representative, please, and make me a good one." This is overcoming stress God's way.

–PEG RANKIN

Leadership Principle

NUMBER 57

STAY FOCUSED ON YOUR MISSION, BUT FLEXIBLE TO YOUR CIRCUMSTANCES AND TO GOD'S SPIRIT.

Are your plans for the day flexible enough to be changed if you sense God taking you down another road?

CAREFUL CUTBACKS

Trimming your staff is one of the hardest things you'll ever have to do as a leader. And strangely, one of the best.

THE WORD FOR THE DAY

THOSE IN GIDEON'S ARMY WHO WERE AFRAID OR NOT READY FOR THE CHALLENGE WOULD HAVE HELD BACK THE EFFORT. PERSONAL ISSUES CAN OFTEN THREATEN THE GREATER GOOD.

———— ❧ ————

FEW THINGS DISRUPT A PERSON'S LIFE LIKE BEING ELIMINATED FROM THEIR JOB. BE VERY SURE YOU HAVE TRIED ALL OTHER OPTIONS FIRST.

———— ❧ ————

CUTTING SOMEONE LOOSE CAN OFTEN BE THE BEST THING FOR THEM. ALMOST INVARIABLY, GOD LEADS THEM TO A BETTER PLACE, A BETTER FIT, ONE THEY WOULD NEVER HAVE CHOSEN ON THEIR OWN.

Judges 7:2-4a, 5-7

The LORD said to Gideon, "You have too many men for me to deliver Midian into their hands. In order that Israel may not boast against me that her own strength has saved her, announce now to the people, 'Anyone who trembles with fear may turn back and leave Mount Gilead.'" So twenty-two thousand men left, while ten thousand remained.

But the LORD said to Gideon, "There are still too many men. Take them down to the water, and I will sift them out for you there. . . .

So Gideon took the men down to the water. There the LORD told him, "Separate those who lap the water with their tongues like a dog from those who kneel down to drink."

Three hundred men lapped with their hands to their mouths. All the rest got down on their knees to drink.

The LORD said to Gideon, "With the three hundred men that lapped I will save you and give the Midianites into your hands. Let all the other men go, each to his own place."

THE VOICE OF WISDOM

It takes a thousand buds to make one American Beauty rose, consequently nine hundred and ninety-nine of them must be suppressed.

Disbudding consists in removing the buds before they have time to grow into young branches. It is a species of pruning which has for its object not only training but also economy in regard to the resources of a tree, in order that there may be a greater supply of nourishment for the development of those buds which are allowed to remain.

If the roots are capable of absorbing only a given quantity of nutritive matter for the supply of all the buds upon a stem, and if a number of those buds be removed, it must be evident that those which remain will be able to draw a greater supply of sap and grow more vigorously than they otherwise would have done. This fact has furnished the idea of *disbudding*. It has been proved that a judicious thinning of the buds after they have been unfolded in spring is a great utility.

–MRS. CHARLES COWMAN

If personnel problems are continuing to side-track you, ask God to show you the wisest way to handle them.

MONEY MATTERS

*Money is neither good nor bad. But leaders who learn how
to manage it wisely can make it work like God intended.*

THE WORD FOR THE DAY

EFFECTIVE MONEY MANAGEMENT
AND HARD WORK ARE COM-
PANION VIRTUES.

GOD IS THE TRUE GIVER OF IT
ALL, BUT HE ENTRUSTS US TO
PROVIDE FOR OURSELVES AND
OUR FAMILIES.

HANDLING MONEY WISELY SETS
A GOOD EXAMPLE FOR OTHERS.

SELF-DISCIPLINE IS THE FIRST
PREREQUISITE FOR FAITHFUL
STEWARDSHIP.

WHENEVER YOU'RE MANAGING
OTHERS' MONEY OR DONA-
TIONS, ALWAYS TREAT IT WITH
THE SAME CARE AS IF IT WERE
YOUR OWN.

2 Thessalonians 3:6-13

In the name of the Lord Jesus Christ, we command you, brothers, to keep away from every brother who is idle and does not live according to the teaching you received from us.

For you yourselves know how you ought to follow our example. We were not idle when we were with you, nor did we eat anyone's food without paying for it. On the contrary, we worked night and day, laboring and toiling so that we would not be a burden to any of you.

We did this, not because we do not have the right to such help, but in order to make ourselves a model for you to follow.

For even when we were with you, we gave you this rule: "If a man will not work, he shall not eat."

We hear that some among you are idle. They are not busy; they are busybodies. Such people we command and urge in the Lord Jesus Christ to settle down and earn the bread they eat.

And as for you, brothers, never tire of doing what is right.

THE VOICE OF WISDOM

Being a woman, I know that I have God-given strengths by virtue of my female genes. I'm a nurturer. I'm more sensitive to detail and able to keep track of where things are and where they're supposed to be. I love to watch things grow. Knowing everyone is safe and tucked in at night somehow gives me a feeling of well-being and security. I think those are characteristics God placed inside of me, and guess what? Those parts of my personality make me the best one to look after our investments. They need to be nurtured, allowed to grow in the safest place possible so they are all cozy and warm.

Stop for a moment and think about how smart, clever, capable, and responsible you are in so many other areas of your life. There is absolutely no reason you cannot add competent money manager and financial planner to your list of abilities and skills.

A financially confident woman is a woman who has the knowledge, ability, and desire to behave in a financially responsible manner.

–MARY HUNT

Leadership & Principle

NUMBER 59

MANAGE YOUR MONEY WITH WISDOM AND INTEGRITY.

Whether your financial world is a household budget or a company spreadsheet, ask God to help you handle it well.

READY FOR ANYTHING

*Leaders know that getting themselves ready to start
the day involves a lot more than deodorant and a doughnut.*

THE WORD FOR THE DAY

PLANNING AHEAD WILL MAKE YOUR DRIVETIME A LOT MORE PEACEFUL, YOUR INNER CONVERSATIONS MORE LIKE PRAYERS AND LESS LIKE REHEARSALS.

———— ∽ ————

"BE DRESSED READY FOR SERVICE," EVEN IF IT REQUIRES GETTING UP A LITTLE EARLIER.

———— ∽ ————

HAVE YOU FIGURED SOME TIME FOR MINISTRY INTO YOUR DAY? AND ARE YOU WILLING TO ADJUST YOUR SCHEDULE IF GOD TAKES YOU IN ANOTHER DIRECTION?

———— ∽ ————

IT'S FAIR TO ASK GOD TO MULTIPLY YOUR TIME AND EFFORTS WHEN UNAVOIDABLE DELAYS HAVE PUT YOUR BEHIND.

Luke 12:35-38, 42-44

"Be dressed ready for service and keep your lamps burning, like men waiting for their master to return from a wedding banquet, so that when he comes and knocks they can immediately open the door for him.

"It will be good for those servants whose master finds them watching when he comes. I tell you the truth, he will dress himself to serve, will have them recline at the table and will come and wait on them.

"It will be good for those servants whose master finds them ready, even if he comes in the second or third watch of the night. . . .

The Lord answered, "Who then is the faithful and wise manager, whom the master puts in charge of his servants to give them their food allowance at the proper time?

"It will be good for that servant whom the master finds doing so when he returns. I tell you the truth, he will put him in charge of all his possessions."

THE VOICE OF WISDOM

I used to feel guilty when, in my busyness, my quiet time would wane into a time for planning, list making, and organizing my day. But somehow, even through the guilt, the activity seemed to have sort of a sacred effect when first thing in the morning I thought over my day and made lists, schedules, and agendas, then prayed about the tasks of the day. I knew it wasn't what all the books said to do in a quiet time, but part of it felt right.

If we included a time for planning in our quiet time, we could orient our entire day toward God instead of trying to find a few moments here and there to squeeze Him in. By including planning as part of our quiet time, four things happen: (1) our devotions are not separated from the rest of our activities, (2) our planning can be done in the context of prayer and God's Word, (3) we affirm constantly our commitment to the purpose and values of the kingdom of God, and (4) we experience the guidance of the Holy Spirit in establishing our priorities and plans.

–DEBBIE LLOYD

Leadership & Principle

NUMBER 60

LEADERS DO THEIR HOMEWORK. THEY ENTER INTO EACH DAY PREPARED.

Trust the heart you have in your daily quiet time more than the voices you hear throughout the rest of the day.

EXPERIENCE TELLS ME

*Good leaders never stop learning. But the best ones try
to avoid having to learn the same lessons over and over again.*

THE WORD FOR THE DAY

ARROGANCE CAN PUMP YOU FULL OF UNWISE, UNCHALLENGED CONCLUSIONS. HUMILITY WILL MAKE YOU LESS LIABLE TO COURT DISASTER.

———— ∽∂∾ ————

"MY EARS HAD HEARD OF YOU BUT NOW MY EYES HAVE SEEN YOU." THERE'S NO SUBSTITUTE FOR SEEING WHAT GOD CAN DO FIRSTHAND.

———— ∽∂∾ ————

THERE IS A SPIRITUAL REWARD TO BEING MEEK BEFORE GOD, BUT A VERY NATURAL REWARD FOR THOSE WHO LEARN FROM THEIR MISTAKES.

———— ∽∂∾ ————

MAKE IT YOUR DESIRE TO DIE "OLD AND FULL OF YEARS," NOT JUST IN AGE, BUT IN WISDOM.

Job 42:1-6, 12-13, 16-17

Then Job replied to the LORD: "I know that you can do all things; no plan of yours can be thwarted.

"You asked, 'Who is this that obscures my counsel without knowledge?' Surely I spoke of things I did not understand, things too wonderful for me to know.

"You said, 'Listen now, and I will speak; I will question you, and you shall answer me.'

"My ears had heard of you but now my eyes have seen you. Therefore I despise myself and repent in dust and ashes..."

The LORD blessed the latter part of Job's life more than the first. He had fourteen thousand sheep, six thousand camels, a thousand yoke of oxen and a thousand donkeys. And he also had seven sons and three daughters....

After this, Job lived a hundred and forty years; he saw his children and their children to the fourth generation.

And so he died, old and full of years.

THE VOICE OF WISDOM

Experience forces theory to work into real life. Experience also gives us insight into what we don't want to do and how we don't want to do it. Experience helps us personalize what we do and gives us a methodology for doing it.

Because I have worked with women in crisis year after year, I now handle them differently from how I did when I was a novice. So often I rushed to fulfill the individual's every need and tried to rescue her from her hurt. In my first few years of ministry, if someone called in a panic over her marriage, I felt I had to run right over and solve her problem.

But I learned that if I always pulled a rescue, she never learned to lean on God when she felt panicked. She often didn't finish taking the steps that would lead to the eradication of the source of the problem; she didn't need to, since I would fix things for her. It isn't always wise to rush right in. If a problem has taken years to develop, it will probably take years (and lots of hard work) to get resolved. I now realize that I shouldn't work harder at her recovery than she is.

–PAM FARREL

Leadership
Principle

NUMBER 61

WISE LEADERS ARE ABLE TO BUILD ON PAST EXPERIENCE.

Keeping a journal you can refer to from a distance is one of the best ways to learn from the past, prepare for the future.

GOALTENDING

Setting goals can eat into your work time.
But trying to work without them will eat away your effectiveness.

THE WORD FOR THE DAY

WE MEASURE OUR LIVES IN YEARS, BUT GOD MEASURES THEM IN DAYS—THE SINGLE STEPS WE TAKE ON THE WAY TO OUR FUTURE.

BE SURE TO ATTACH ACTIONS TO YOUR GOALS SO YOU DON'T REMAIN FOREVER STUCK IN THE PLANNING STAGE.

YOU'LL NEED OTHERS TO HELP YOU ACHIEVE YOUR GOALS. DON'T TRY TO DO IT ALL YOURSELF. SHARE THE DREAM, THE LOAD, AND THE REWARD.

KEEP THE END GOAL IN SIGHT AT ALL TIMES. THEN YOU'LL KNOW WHEN YOU GET THERE.

1 Kings 6:1-2, 11-13, 37-38

In the four hundred and eightieth year after the Israelites had come out of Egypt, in the fourth year of Solomon's reign over Israel, in the month of Ziv, the second month, he began to build the temple of the LORD.

The temple that King Solomon built for the LORD was sixty cubits long, twenty wide and thirty high. . . .

The word of the LORD came to Solomon: "As for this temple you are building, if you follow my decrees, carry out my regulations and keep all my commands and obey them, I will fulfill through you the promise I gave to David your father. And I will live among the Israelites and will not abandon my people Israel. . . ."

The foundation of the temple of the LORD was laid in the fourth year, in the month of Ziv.

In the eleventh year in the month of Bul, the eighth month, the temple was finished in all its details according to its specifications. He had spent seven years building it.

THE VOICE OF WISDOM

A good farmer will have his whole year planned. He knows exactly when to plow and sow and harvest and mend the fences and feed the animals. He has daily, weekly, monthly, and yearly goals that he sets for himself and his helpers. Then he gets up in the morning with one thought in mind: to accomplish what he has planned. He sets realistic goals and then goes to work. Each day he accomplishes just a little, so at harvest time his family's table is set for another year.

We've recently noticed that the things that have the most impact on our lives are those that require diligent, consistent effort–just one or two steps a day. Things like diet, exercise, changing old habits, Bible study, and prayer. Chasing fantasies is like always hoping something will save us from our circumstances–like winning the lottery–rather than realizing that our circumstances are from the Lord.

Set for yourself worthwhile goals in your life, then work toward them diligently. God honors goals, and will take you places with them you never thought possible–one little step at a time.

–AMY BEASLEY

Leadership Principle

NUMBER 62

SET AMBITIOUS GOALS AND MONITOR YOUR PROGRESS REGULARLY.

What is God asking of you? Put it into words, then put it to a plan– then watch Him help you put it into action.

PURE MOTIVATION

Every leader has people who are aggravating and hard to motivate.
But when you lead with love, good things follow.

THE WORD FOR THE DAY

JESUS HAD EVERY REASON TO SEE NOTHING BUT THE BAD IN HIS RAG-TAG GROUP OF FOLLOWERS, BUT HE CHOSE TO LOVE THEM INSTEAD.

⎯⎯ ⬤ ⎯⎯

FRIENDS. IS THAT HOW YOU FEEL ABOUT THOSE WHO ANSWER TO YOU?

⎯⎯ ⬤ ⎯⎯

HELPING PEOPLE "BEAR FRUIT—FRUIT THAT WILL LAST" SHOULD BE THE PRIMARY GOAL OF YOUR MOTIVATIONAL STRATEGIES. PRODUCTIVE INDIVIDUALS RESULT IN A PRODUCTIVE WHOLE.

⎯⎯ ⬤ ⎯⎯

GENUINE LOVE FOR OTHERS HAS A WAY OF BEING CONTAGIOUS. IF YOU START THE PROCESS, PEOPLE WILL FOLLOW.

John 15:9-17

"As the Father has loved me, so have I loved you. Now remain in my love. If you obey my commands, you will remain in my love, just as I have obeyed my Father's commands and remain in his love.

"I have told you this so that my joy may be in you and that your joy may be complete. My command is this: Love each other as I have loved you.

"Greater love has no one than this, that he lay down his life for his friends. You are my friends if you do what I command.

"I no longer call you servants, because a servant does not know his master's business. Instead, I have called you friends, for everything that I learned from my Father I have made known to you.

"You did not choose me, but I chose you and appointed you to go and bear fruit—fruit that will last. Then the Father will give you whatever you ask in my name. This is my command: Love each other."

THE VOICE OF WISDOM

There are many ways of motivating people to do something you wish them to do. During the Industrial Revolution in this country, people were hired on a "piece work" basis. The more work they turned out, the more pay they received.

Other motivational methods used by secular leadership included threats, humiliation, and anger. When all of these failed, manipulation became the next method. By cheering the successful performer with applause, plaques, and public commendation, it was thought that everyone would be motivated to do a better job.

Now we know that people are "turned on" most successfully when their motivation is internal. And the most common internal need is to be loved. Some contemporary leaders now feel that a caring, sympathetic, empathetic attitude is the most successful way to motivate others.

A Christian leader will succeed if she convinces her followers that God–as well as she herself–recognizes and honors the person's strengths and abilities, and that each worker has something of value to offer others.

–LINDA MCGINN

Leadership Principle

NUMBER 63

TRUE LEADERS MOTIVATE WITHOUT MANIPULATING.

Ask God to help you love those under your leadership, even the ones who cause you the most trouble.

WHAT DO *YOU* THINK?

*People look to you for making good decisions and handling tough issues.
Do you look to anyone to help you do it well?*

THE WORD FOR THE DAY

"PLANS FAIL FOR LACK OF
COUNSEL, BUT WITH MANY
ADVISERS THEY SUCCEED"
(PROVERBS 15:22).

———— ❧ ————

YOU HAVE TOO MANY DECI-
SIONS TO MAKE IN A DAY TO
THINK YOU WILL ALWAYS
KNOW WHAT IS BEST
ON YOUR OWN.

———— ❧ ————

SOME MATTERS DO REQUIRE
IMMEDIATE ACTION, BUT NOT
EVERYTHING THAT SCREAMS
DESERVES AN ABRUPT DECI-
SION. WAITING IS OFTEN THE
BEST COURSE OF ACTION.

———— ❧ ————

REHOBOAM LATER REJECTED
THE ELDERS' ADVICE IN FAVOR
OF HIS FRIENDS' WORDS.
COVET THE COMPANY
OF WISE ADVISORS.

1 Kings 12:1-7

Rehoboam went to Shechem, for all the Israelites had gone there to make him king.

When Jeroboam son of Nebat heard this (he was still in Egypt, where he had fled from King Solomon), he returned from Egypt.

So they sent for Jeroboam, and he and the whole assembly of Israel went to Rehoboam and said to him: "Your father put a heavy yoke on us, but now lighten the harsh labor and the heavy yoke he put on us, and we will serve you."

Rehoboam answered, "Go away for three days and then come back to me." So the people went away.

Then King Rehoboam consulted the elders who had served his father Solomon during his lifetime. "How would you advise me to answer these people?" he asked.

They replied, "If today you will be a servant to these people and serve them and give them a favorable answer, they will always be your servants."

THE VOICE OF WISDOM

In a relationship where there is transparency, there can be enormous growth. For as the windows become unshaded, we permit others to offer light to our opinions, our concerns, and our dreams. They help complete our thoughts, balance our extremes, and correct our miscalculations. They remind us of parallel situations that we may have forgotten and that now bring encouragement, direction, or prevention. They may have shared with us the very keys of life, which may escalate our maturity or protect us from destruction. But transparency has to happen first.

When the architect first came to Plato with his offer to build a private house, he thought he had a very special thing to offer. But Plato saw it all differently. A healthy life in a home is a transparent one, he believed. And that demands more windows than walls. What Plato knew about homes, we must learn about relationships. The question is: Are we building walls or opening windows?

–GAIL MACDONALD

Leaning on the advice of others can multiply your skills in using sound judgment. Be humble enough to let them help.

A MATTER OF PRINCIPLE

If your core convictions are firmly in place before times of crisis hit, they will still be standing when the crisis is over.

THE WORD FOR THE DAY

THE FIRST STEP INTO COMPROMISE IS A STEP IN THE WRONG DIRECTION. YOU WILL NEVER REGRET DOING WHAT YOU KNEW WAS RIGHT.

———— ❧ ————

GODLY PRINCIPLES GIVE YOU LIGHT TO SEE IMPORTANT THINGS THAT OTHERS OVERLOOK.

———— ❧ ————

"ABOVE ALL ELSE, GUARD YOUR HEART"—YOUR MOTIVES, YOUR INTENTIONS. THEY REVEAL WHO YOU REALLY ARE, AND DETERMINE THE KIND OF LEADER YOU BECOME.

———— ❧ ————

LOOK AT YOUR LIFE AND LEADERSHIP AS A LONG ROAD, BUT WITH DAILY DECISIONS THAT AFFECT ITS OUTCOME.

Proverbs 4:13-19, 23-27

Hold on to instruction, do not let it go; guard it well, for it is your life. Do not set foot on the path of the wicked or walk in the way of evil men. Avoid it, do not travel on it; turn from it and go on your way. For they cannot sleep till they do evil; they are robbed of slumber till they make someone fall. They eat the bread of wickedness and drink the wine of violence.

The path of the righteous is like the first gleam of dawn, shining ever brighter till the full light of day. But the way of the wicked is like deep darkness; they do not know what makes them stumble. . . .

Above all else, guard your heart, for it is the wellspring of life. Put away perversity from your mouth; keep corrupt talk far from your lips.

Let your eyes look straight ahead, fix your gaze directly before you. Make level paths for your feet and take only ways that are firm. Do not swerve to the right or the left; keep your foot from evil.

THE VOICE OF WISDOM

Consider well what a separation from the world, what purity, what devotion, what exemplary virtue, are required in those who are to guide others to glory.

I would advise you to arrange your affairs by a certain method, by which means you will learn to improve every precious moment. Begin and end the day with Him who is the Alpha and Omega, and if you really experience what it is to love God, you will redeem all the time you can for His more immediate service.

Endeavor to act upon principle and do not live like the rest of mankind, who pass through the world like straws upon a river, which are carried which way the stream or wind drive them. Get as deep an impression on your mind as is possible of the constant presence of the great and holy God. He is about our beds and about our paths and spies out all our ways. Whenever you are tempted to the commission of any sin, or the omission of any duty, pause and say to yourself, What am I about to do? God sees me.

–SUSANNA WESLEY

Leadership Principle

NUMBER 65

CHRISTIAN LEADERS OPERATE FROM CLEARLY DEFINED BIBLICAL PRINCIPLES.

Principle is bigger than burnout, stronger than stress, tougher than temper. Let God's ways rule everything.

GENEROUS HELPINGS

Along with the responsibility of creating and generating comes the blessed responsibility of giving something back.

THE WORD FOR THE DAY

THE CORINTHIANS HAD PLEDGED TO SUPPORT THE JERUSALEM CHURCH BUT HAD BACKED OUT ON THEIR PROMISE. FOLLOW THROUGH ON YOUR COMMITMENTS.

❧

YOUR GENEROSITY HAS EVERYDAY OPPORTUNITIES TO EXPRESS ITSELF. AND LIFELONG REWARDS.

❧

INDIVIDUALS ARE COMMANDED TO TITHE. WHY SHOULDN'T COMPANIES DO THE SAME?

❧

A WATCHING WORLD WANTS TO SEE HOW CHRISTIANS HANDLE THEIR MONEY. DOES YOUR EXAMPLE SHOW THAT MONEY DOESN'T HAVE A HOLD ON YOU?

2 Corinthians 9:6-8, 10-11, 13a

Remember this: Whoever sows sparingly will also reap sparingly, and whoever sows generously will also reap generously.

Each man should give what he has decided in his heart to give, not reluctantly or under compulsion, for God loves a cheerful giver.

And God is able to make all grace abound to you, so that in all things at all times, having all that you need, you will abound in every good work. . . .

Now he who supplies seed to the sower and bread for food will also supply and increase your store of seed and will enlarge the harvest of your righteousness.

You will be made rich in every way so that you can be generous on every occasion, and through us your generosity will result in thanksgiving to God. . . .

Because of the service by which you have proved yourselves, men will praise God for the obedience that accompanies your confession of the gospel of Christ.

THE VOICE OF WISDOM

Leadership Principle

NUMBER 66

LEADERS SHOULD BE GENEROUS WITH THEIR TIME AND MONEY.

I give to God because I love Him and because I am grateful beyond belief for all that He has done for me every day of my life. Giving from a grateful heart and expecting nothing in return is a sweet offering to the One who owns everything I have anyway. It's the very least I can do. And as I give, I experience God's grace.

If you've never been one to habitually give, get ready to experience a whole new dimension in your life. I don't know of anything that will take your eyes off your own situation faster than giving to others.

If you want your life to have purpose, your finances to come into balance, and your faith increased, become a giver!

I would strongly suggest you add this to your personal belief system: *Part of everything I have is mine to give away.* If you really believe that, your attitudes will begin to reflect it, your behavior will change, and your life will be greatly enriched. I firmly believe that as we prove ourselves to be responsible with our resources, more and more resources will be entrusted to us to handle faithfully.

–MARY HUNT

You've worked hard, yet you've been given much to get to this point in leadership. Bless as you've been blessed.

NO COMPROMISE

There are times when taking a short cut in leadership makes so much sense, but is still so much disobedience to God.

THE WORD FOR THE DAY

FROM THE INSTRUCTIONS OF EXODUS 25, THE ARK WAS TO BE CARRIED ON POLES, NOT ON A CART. UZZAH'S DEATH WAS THE RESULT, NOT OF A REFLEX ACTION, BUT AN EARLIER DISOBEDIENCE.

———— ∞ ————

IF YOU WOULDN'T WANT JESUS WATCHING YOU DO IT, DON'T DO IT.

———— ∞ ————

PROCEDURES BECOME OUTDATED, BUT CHANGE THEM ONLY AFTER CAREFUL REVIEW. OTHERS BEFORE YOU MAY HAVE ASKED THE SAME QUESTIONS YOU'RE ASKING NOW, BUT FOUND THE FLAW IN YOUR LOGIC.

———— ∞ ————

"ABSTAIN FROM ALL APPEARANCE OF EVIL" (1 THESSALONIANS 5:22)

2 Samuel 6:3-9

They set the ark of God on a new cart and brought it from the house of Abinadab, which was on the hill. Uzzah and Ahio, sons of Abinadab, were guiding the new cart with the ark of God on it, and Ahio was walking in front of it.

David and the whole house of Israel were celebrating with all their might before the LORD, with songs and with harps, lyres, tambourines, sistrums and cymbals.

When they came to the threshing floor of Nacon, Uzzah reached out and took hold of the ark of God, because the oxen stumbled.

The LORD's anger burned against Uzzah because of his irreverent act; therefore God struck him down and he died there beside the ark of God.

Then David was angry because the LORD's wrath had broken out against Uzzah, and to this day that place is called Perez Uzzah.

David was afraid of the LORD that day and said, "How can the ark of the LORD ever come to me?"

THE VOICE OF WISDOM

There was a time when our ethical standards were formed at home. But with so much of our population in the work force, leaders in all occupations and professions have more moral and ethical responsibility than ever before.

Our occupational leaders must have the courage to speak out for ethical behavior and justice. Indifference or silence to unethical behavior demoralizes people, destroys organizations, and strangles our nation.

In these days of mergers, acquisitions, and corporate takeovers, we read and hear so much about unethical behavior. It exists on an alarming scale. It makes headlines that sell newspapers and boost newscast ratings. But this sensational unethical behavior is *not* the norm. There are hundreds and thousands of ethical business transactions conducted every day by ethical men and women. We must be sure that we do not become desensitized to unethical behavior because we see and hear so much about it. If we are going to make a difference, it is critical that we set the example of high ethics for others to follow.

–SHEILA MURRAY BETHEL

Leadership Principle

NUMBER 67

LEADERS MUST NOT TAKE SHORT CUTS OR BREAK THE RULES EVEN FROM GOOD MOTIVES.

Bending a rule may be the only way you see to help you handle your latest problem. But you're only asking for more.

FEAR OF TRYING

When problems pile up faster than you can handle them,
that's when leaders make sure they've hidden the panic button.

THE WORD FOR THE DAY

STORMS SPRING UP OFTEN IN THE LEADER'S LIFE, MANY TIMES WITHOUT WARNING. GET YOUR PROBLEM-SOLVING STRATEGIES READY BEFORE THE WORST HITS.

JESUS DIDN'T AVOID THE PROBLEM OR MAKE LIGHT OF HIS FRIENDS' FEARS. HE JUST HANDLED THE SITUATION. LEADERS JUST HANDLE IT.

THERE IS A CALM PLACE IN THE MIDST OF EVERY TRYING SITUATION. AND IT'S NEAR TO THE HEART OF GOD.

FEARFUL SITUATIONS GIVE YOUR FAITH A CHANCE TO PROVE ITS LOFTY WORDS.

Mark 4:35–41

That day when evening came, he said to his disciples, "Let us go over to the other side."

Leaving the crowd behind, they took him along just as he was, in the boat. There were also other boats with him.

A furious squall came up, and the waves broke over the boat, so that it was nearly swamped.

Jesus was in the stern, sleeping on a cushion. The disciples woke him and said to him, "Teacher, don't you care if we drown?"

He got up, rebuked the wind and said to the waves, "Quiet! Be still!" Then the wind died down and it was completely calm.

He said to his disciples, "Why are you so afraid? Do you still have no faith?"

They were terrified and asked each other, "Who is this? Even the wind and the waves obey him!"

THE VOICE OF WISDOM

First and foremost, we must learn to respond instead of react. When we react–act on our first impulse–we often cause ourselves and others more trouble. We simply need to take the time to think through how to solve the problem that's confronting us.

One thing I'm pretty good at is putting problems through the enlarging machine. That's when we lie awake reviewing situations like one lost client. Somehow we move from a fairly insignificant occurrence to scenes from a soap opera: We're never going to work in our profession again. We're going to go broke, lose the house, or use up all our retirement. When we're working the enlarging machine, the last thing we think of doing is responding creatively by going out and finding a new client, or calling on the one we lost to see if there's a possibility of a turnabout.

Responding is a different kettle of fish. Responding is a slower process. It demands that we listen carefully, that we examine and often adjust our attitude, and that we calmly look at possible approaches to solving the problem before we take action.

–KATHY PEEL

Leadership Principle

NUMBER 68

LEADERS ARE NOT FEARLESS, BUT DO NOT LET FEAR DICTATE THEIR THINKING.

You probably have two or three situations swirling around you that need your immediate attention. Act, don't react.

CRITICAL SITUATIONS

*It's easy to find fault with those in leadership,
but not to find leaders who can find forgiveness in their hearts.*

THE WORD FOR THE DAY

IT IS BETTER TO SUFFER UNJUSTLY THAN TO SEEK YOUR OWN REVENGE.

❧

THE BIBLICAL PRINCIPLE OF "SECOND MILE" SERVICE MEANS DOING MORE THAN EXPECTED, WHETHER IT MEANS TAKING A SHORTER LUNCH OR WEARING A LONGER FUSE.

❧

LEADERSHIP INVITES OPPOSITION. SO WRITE THIS IN STONE AND KEEP IT OUT WHERE YOU CAN ALWAYS REMEMBER IT. "LOVE YOUR ENEMIES."

❧

WORDS FROM PEOPLE YOU DON'T PARTICULARLY LIKE CAN BE HARD TO HEAR. BUT LISTEN ANYWAY. THERE MAY BE SOME TRUTH IN THEM.

Matthew 5:38-41, 43-48

"You have heard that it was said, 'Eye for eye and tooth for tooth.'

"But I tell you, Do not resist an evil person. I someone strikes you on the right cheek, turn to him the other also.

"And if someone wants to sue you and take your tunic, let him have your cloak as well. I someone forces you to go one mile, go with him two miles....

"You have heard that it was said, 'Love your neighbor and hate your enemy.'

"But I tell you: Love your enemies and pray for those who persecute you, that you may be sons of your Father in heaven. He causes his sun to rise on the evil and the good, and sends rain on the righteous and the unrighteous.

"If you love those who love you, what reward will you get? Are not even the tax collectors doing that?

"And if you greet only your brothers, what are you doing more than others? Do not even pagans do that?"

Be perfect, therefore, as your heavenly Father is perfect.

THE VOICE OF WISDOM

Leadership Principle

NUMBER 69

LEADERS KNOW THAT SOME CRITICISM SHOULD BE HEEDED, SOME SHOULD BE IGNORED.

One day a letter landed on my desk. A long letter, full of attacks on my character, my motives, my ministry, and my family. Usually I can deal quickly with criticism, but this was such a personal attack. It followed a long stretch of exhausting work, so I was very vulnerable to discouragement. As I read the letter, a dark cloud covered my heart. I cried out to God in my hurt. Then I got angry. Then I cried. Then I got depressed. I felt as if I were having an emotional knock-down, drag-out fight.

Satan wanted me so discouraged that I couldn't minister. And believe me, my flesh felt like giving in. I knew I could choose either a bitter place or a broken place. It's natural to want to turn bitter. It's better to be broken over a hurt and allow God to heal it.

It took several months, but gradually my perspective returned. In my brokenness, I continued to do what God had called me to do. As I placed my eyes on Jesus and the needy world around me, a new, bolder resolve fortified my character. Keep your eyes on God, His opinion, and His plan. Healing happens as you continue in your passion.

–PAM FARREL

If you're under the unkind words of criticism, try not to take it too personally. And try to take it to the Lord first.

YES, YOU WILL

*No matter what kind of leadership post you fill,
you can hold your staff to a solid work ethic and value system.*

THE WORD FOR THE DAY

THE BIBLE MAY OR MAY NOT BE AN ACCEPTED FORM OF AUTHORITY IN YOUR LEADER-SHIP ARENA. BUT ITS PRINCI-PLES WORK ANYWHERE, WITH ANYBODY.

〜〜〜

YOU CAN'T CONTROL THE WAY PEOPLE LIVE WHEN THEY'RE AWAY FROM WORK, BUT YOU CAN DEMAND A HIGH LEVEL OF HONOR AND ACCOUNTABILITY WHEN THEY'RE WITH YOU.

〜〜〜

YOUR LOFTY EXPECTATIONS ARE DOING PEOPLE A GREATER SERVICE THAN THEY TRULY REALIZE. NO MATTER HOW MUCH FLAK YOU GET, STAY CONFIDENT YOU'RE DOING WHAT'S BEST FOR THEM.

2 Timothy 2:1-6, 15, 22

You then, my son, be strong in the grace that is in Christ Jesus.

And the things you have heard me say in the presence of many witnesses entrust to reliable men who will also be qualified to teach others.

Endure hardship with us like a good soldier of Christ Jesus.

No one serving as a soldier gets involved in civilian affairs—he wants to please his commanding officer.

Similarly, if anyone competes as an athlete, he does not receive the victor's crown unless he competes according to the rules. The hardworking farmer should be the first to receive a share of the crops. . . .

Do your best to present yourself to God as one approved, a workman who does not need to be ashamed and who correctly handles the word of truth. . . .

Flee the evil desires of youth, and pursue righteousness, faith, love and peace, along with those who call on the Lord out of a pure heart.

THE VOICE OF WISDOM

Every Christian woman has opportunities to lead. In the home, church, community, or marketplace, our various relationships offer potent possibilities to show the way and to stimulate to action.

Leadership & Principle

NUMBER 70

LEADERS HAVE A RIGHT TO EXPECT INTEGRITY FROM THE PEOPLE WHO SERVE UNDER THEM.

But first, we must recognize that without the internal motivation of the Holy Spirit, we can–at best–only elicit short-term behavioral change. Only God's Holy Spirit can replace the "heart of stone" with the "heart of flesh" (Ezekiel 36:26). When God extends His grace and changes a heart of stone to a heart of flesh, the recipient of that grace will be ready to follow and able to learn a new way of life.

Christian women are often blocked from maximizing their potential because they do not understand the power of the Holy Spirit within them. Many Christian women struggle with the I'm-not-good-enough-smart-enough-talented-enough syndrome. A leader of women understands that every daughter of the King has been uniquely designed and equipped for a purpose. She helps women embrace this perspective about themselves, then challenges them to squeeze every ounce of potential out of each ability and situation.

–SUSAN HUNT

High standards not only make people better workers, but better people. And isn't that what you're hoping for?

THE LITTLE THINGS

The greatness that people see in you is simply a result of your daily faithfulness. God will always honor that in you.

THE WORD FOR THE DAY

YOUR REACH AND INFLUENCE HAS BEEN ENTRUSTED TO YOU BY GOD. GUARD WELL YOUR CALLING AND THE PEOPLE YOU SERVE WITHIN IT.

DON'T WORRY ABOUT WHAT YOU DON'T HAVE. MAKE THE BEST WITH WHAT YOU DO.

YOU MAY NOT BE IN THE POSITION YOU WANT TO BE, BUT BY SERVING IN IT FAITHFULLY, YOU CAN MAKE THIS A PROFITABLE SEASON OF LIFE.

YES, DO THE LITTLE THINGS WELL, BUT DON'T LET YOUR LARGER VISION GET BOGGED DOWN IN THE DETAILS.

Matthew 25:14-21

"Again, it will be like a man going on a journey, who called his servants and entrusted his property to them.

"To one he gave five talents of money, to another two talents, and to another one talent, each according to his ability. Then he went on his journey.

"The man who had received the five talents went at once and put his money to work and gained five more. So also, the one with the two talents gained two more. But the man who had received the one talent went off, dug a hole in the ground and hid his master's money.

"After a long time the master of those servants returned and settled accounts with them. The man who had received the five talents brought the other five. 'Master,' he said, 'you entrusted me with five talents. See, I have gained five more.'

"His master replied, 'Well done, good and faithful servant! You have been faithful with a few things; I will put you in charge of many things. Come and share your master's happiness!'"

THE VOICE OF WISDOM

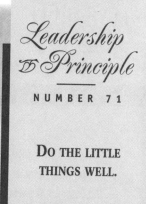

Leadership & Principle

NUMBER 71

DO THE LITTLE THINGS WELL.

The overcoming of one difficulty makes easier the conquering of the next until finally we are almost invincible. Success actually becomes a habit through the determined overcoming of obstacles as we meet them one by one.

If we are not being successful, a change in our fortunes can be brought by making a start, however small, in the right direction and then following it up.

For some reason, of course, according to some universal law, we gather momentum as we proceed in whatever way we go, and by overcoming a small difficulty, we are more able to conquer the next, though greater. So if we allow ourselves to fail, it is easier to fail the next time, and failure becomes a habit, making us unable to look a difficulty fairly in the face, but to turn and run from it.

There is no elation equal to the rise of the spirit to meet and overcome a difficulty, not with a foolish overconfidence, but by keeping things in their proper relations by praying, now and then, the prayer of a good fighter whom I used to know: "Lord, make me sufficient to mine own occasion."

–LAURA INGALLS WILDER

If you're saving your best efforts for the next big thing, you'll miss a lot of opportunities to prepare yourself for it.

OUTSIDE THE BOX

Some days you wish you could just go through the motions
and fill in the blanks. But you've been called higher than that.

THE WORD FOR THE DAY

CHALLENGE THE RUT OF
UNQUESTIONED EXPECTATIONS
WITH THE FRESH AIR OF A
NEW APPROACH.

———— ❧ ————

YOU NEVER KNOW WHO WILL
BE OPEN TO YOUR IDEAS.
MAKE A GOOD CASE FOR IT,
AND THEY JUST MIGHT LISTEN.

———— ❧ ————

TV AND TALK SHOWS ASK
NOTHING OF YOUR BRAIN.
CHOOSE RECREATIONAL ACTIVI-
TIES THAT CHANGE YOUR PACE,
BUT STIMULATE YOUR MIND.

———— ❧ ————

DON'T BE AFRAID TO ACT ON
YOUR HUNCHES.

———— ❧ ————

TWEAKS AND ADJUSTMENTS
ALONG THE WAY CAN AVOID
YOUR NEED FOR A
TOTAL OVERHAUL.

Numbers 27:1-8

The daughters of Zelophehad . . . belonged to the clans of Manasseh son of Joseph. The names of the daughters were Mahlah, Noah, Hoglah, Milcah and Tirzah.

They approached the entrance to the Tent of Meeting and stood before Moses, Eleazar the priest, the leaders and the whole assembly, and said,

"Our father died in the desert. He was not among Korah's followers, who banded together against the LORD, but he died for his own sin and left no sons. Why should our father's name disappear from his clan because he had no son? Give us property among our father's relatives."

So Moses brought their case before the LORD and the LORD said to him, "What Zelophehad's daughters are saying is right. You must certainly give them property as an inheritance among their father's relatives and give their father's inheritance over to them.

"Say to the Israelites, 'If a man dies and leaves no son, give his inheritance over to his daughter.'"

THE VOICE OF WISDOM

Women have always been able to make do with what life hands them, to create an ordered universe in the midst of chaos and stress. Women have always been able to make something from nothing, stretching the stew, making the worn-out clothes or opportunities into something new, smiling and caressing in spite of their own inclination to give in to tears and fatigue. Yet, while their hands were performing the task at hand, their minds were racing on. Assimilating. Analyzing. Philosophizing.

So much of men's thinking is applied directly to their work. The result of their thinking is output, income, product. But much of what women think about does not create tangible product. Instead, they ponder the meaning and quality of life. Such pondering may not result in consumable products, but it can produce great souls who ask why instead of merely what and how. Women, after all, are about the industry of the heart.

–GLORIA GAITHER

Leadership Principle

NUMBER 72

LEADERS MUST THINK CREATIVELY, BEYOND THE ORDINARY AND EXPECTED.

Stay constantly on the lookout for those in your organization who are showing signs of something greater.

HIGH MINDED

You should have a lot more in your sights than the next big deadline.
Looking back, it won't seem quite so important.

THE WORD FOR THE DAY

THE PROBLEMS AND ISSUES YOU FACED TEN YEARS AGO SEEM SMALL TO YOU NOW. IMAGINE HOW SMALL TODAY'S WILL SEEM . . . FOREVER FROM NOW.

———— ❧ ————

DON'T MAKE GOD HAVE TO TAKE SOMETHING FROM YOU BEFORE YOU REALIZE HOW VALUABLE IT IS.

———— ❧ ————

THE TRAITS OF AN ETERNITY-MINDED PERSON ARE LOVE, PATIENCE, FORGIVENESS, PEACEFULNESS, GRATITUDE. ALL THE GOOD THINGS.

———— ❧ ————

"'YES, I AM COMING SOON.' AMEN. COME, LORD JESUS"

(REVELATION 22:20)

Colossians 3:1-4, 12-15

Since, then, you have been raised with Christ, set your hearts on things above, where Christ is seated at the right hand of God.

Set your minds on things above, not on earthly things. For you died, and your life is now hidden with Christ in God. When Christ, who is your life, appears, then you also will appear with him in glory. . . .

Therefore, as God's chosen people, holy and dearly loved, clothe yourselves with compassion, kindness, humility, gentleness and patience.

Bear with each other and forgive whatever grievances you may have against one another. Forgive as the Lord forgave you.

And over all these virtues put on love, which binds them all together in perfect unity.

Let the peace of Christ rule in your hearts, since as members of one body you were called to peace. And be thankful.

THE VOICE OF WISDOM

It is a feast for me to be in Holland, for I meet friends of former days. At one of these gatherings, I missed one of my friends. Somebody told me, "She is ill. She could not come."

Leadership Principle

NUMBER 73

SUCCESSFUL LEADERS VIEW THEIR TASKS FROM AN ETERNAL PERSPECTIVE.

So I went to see her, and she told me what happened. "I have been very ill, and everyone–myself, too– thought I would die. But then I began to recover."

"Are you happy?"

"Yes. There is much work for me to do in this world. I believe I will return to my everyday life richer than I was before I was ill. I believe I will take the good opportunities which the Lord will give me in the future with more thankfulness, because I thought I had lost them forever. I will see the smaller problems of life in the light of eternity. I thank God that I had this illness. It made me more ready for life."

The Lord never makes a mistake. One day, when we are in heaven, I'm sure we shall see the answers to all the *whys*. My, how often I have asked, "*Why?*" In heaven, we shall see God's side of the embroidery.

God has no problems, only plans. There is never panic in heaven.

–CORRIE TEN BOOM

It seems trite, but it's just so true. Try to view this day with the perspective that you may not get this chance again.

ENCOURAGING WORDS

*Some people are able to rise to a challenge. But everyone stands
a little taller when they feel genuinely appreciated.*

T H E   W O R D   F O R   T H E   D A Y

PAUL'S LETTERS ALMOST
ALWAYS BEGIN WITH AN
ENCOURAGING WORD—EVEN
TO THE STRUGGLING CHURCHES.
THERE'S ALWAYS SOMETHING
GOOD YOU CAN SAY.

———— ❧ ————

LETTERS, NOTES, AND CARDS
CAN TOUCH THE HEART EVEN
MORE THAN THE
SPOKEN WORD.

———— ❧ ————

PRAYER AND ENCOURAGEMENT
OFTEN GO TOGETHER. WHEN
YOU TELL SOMEONE YOU'RE
PRAYING FOR THEM, MAKE
SURE YOU DO.

———— ❧ ————

THE ULTIMATE GOAL OF PAUL'S
ENCOURAGEMENT WAS TO HELP
PEOPLE WANT TO LIVE HOLY
LIVES FOR THE LORD.

1 Thessalonians 3:6-12

*Timothy has just now come to us from you and
has brought good news about your faith and love.
He has told us that you always have pleasant
memories of us and that you long to see us, just
as we also long to see you.*

*Therefore, brothers, in all our distress and per-
secution we were encouraged about you because
of your faith.*

*For now we really live, since you are standing
firm in the Lord.*

*How can we thank God enough for you in
return for all the joy we have in the presence of
our God because of you?*

*Night and day we pray most earnestly that we
may see you again and supply what is lacking in
your faith.*

*Now may our God and Father himself and our
Lord Jesus clear the way for us to come to you.
May the Lord make your love increase and overflow for each other and for everyone else, just as
ours does for you.*

THE VOICE OF WISDOM

I hurried into the ladies' room on my way to the seminar. My husband and I were in Atlanta for a conference including several excellent speakers, including Gordon and Gail MacDonald. In the three years since we had seen them, a lot had happened.

I literally ran into Gail at the sink. After a brief greeting, her first question was, "How is Justin adjusting to your recent move? I've prayed for him."

Amid the hundreds of people she knows, she remembered that our eldest son is handicapped and finds change difficult. Her concern encouraged me. But it did not surprise me.

Eight years prior, I had read her words in *High Call, High Privilege* which admonished Christian leaders in the discipline of learning people's names: "Haven't you told people you really love them when you remember even their children's names?"

Now here I was on the receiving end of that love from an older woman I respect and admire. I realized how essential the power of encouragement is for any woman who truly wants to have an impact on her world.

–LUCINDA SECREST MCDOWELL

Leadership Principle

NUMBER 74

LEADERS WHO ARE MOTIVATED TO ENCOURAGE OTHERS ARE THE ONES WHO MOTIVATE THE BEST.

You may have to go out of your way to give someone an encouraging word. But it'll be worth every step you take.

AGREE TO DISAGREE

*After knocking heads together enough times,
there are certain situations where the best path is to part paths.*

THE WORD FOR THE DAY

THE BIBLE HELPS US REMEMBER THAT THESE PEOPLE WERE ONLY HUMAN. WHO CAN'T RELATE TO HAVING "SUCH A SHARP DISAGREEMENT?"

———— ❧ ————

SEPARATION SHOULD BE A LAST RESORT. FIRST, SEEK COMMON GROUND.

———— ❧ ————

IT IS A FAULTY EXPECTATION THAT BELIEVES WE'LL ALWAYS GET ALONG WITH OTHER. CONFLICT SHOULDN'T BE A SURPRISE.

———— ❧ ————

PAUL AND BARNABAS LATER WORKED TOGETHER AGAIN. AND JOHN MARK FINALLY REGAINED PAUL'S CONFIDENCE. GOODBYES ARE NOT FOREVER. DON'T BURN YOUR BRIDGES ALONG THE WAY.

Acts 15:36-41
Matthew 10:34-36

Some time later Paul said to Barnabas, "Let us go back and visit the brothers in all the towns where we preached the word of the Lord and see how they are doing."

Barnabas wanted to take John, also called Mark, with them, but Paul did not think it wise to take him, because he had deserted them in Pamphylia and had not continued with them in the work.

They had such a sharp disagreement that they parted company. Barnabas took Mark and sailed for Cyprus, but Paul chose Silas and left, commended by the brothers to the grace of the Lord.

He went through Syria and Cilicia, strengthening the churches. . . .

"Do not suppose that I have come to bring peace to the earth. I did not come to bring peace, but a sword.

"For I have come to turn 'a man against his father, a daughter against her mother, a daughter-in-law against her mother-in-law– a man's enemies will be the members of his own household.'"

THE VOICE OF WISDOM

Conflict isn't something we should necessarily be ashamed of, because conflict can lead to better decisions and problem solving. Conflict can also be a benefit when it stretches us intellectually and emotionally.

But some differences may not need to be resolved. Both sides may be right, as early New Testament missionaries Paul and Barnabas discovered. Their conflict over whether to take John Mark along with them eventually led to the same goals. Although John Mark hadn't been exactly what they'd needed on their first missionary journey, Barnabas believed in giving him a second chance. People need second chances. Barnabas was right.

But so was Paul. Perhaps he felt that time to spread the gospel was short, that they didn't have time to waste on encouraging or training the younger, less-committed workers. Paul and his future circumstances–prison, stonings, beatings–demanded nothing less than total commitment.

Two sides can be right. Paul and Barnabas accepted that, and each went his own way.

–DIANNA BOOHER

Some things are worth fighting for. Some things are not. Ask God to help you know how to tell the difference.

CLEARING THE ERROR

Part of working with people is being hurt by them.
But to play your part as a leader, you must be the first to forgive.

THE WORD FOR THE DAY

WATCH JOSEPH'S BROTHERS RETURN TO THEIR TRICKERY. EVEN IN FORGIVING, YOU MAY NEED TO WITHHOLD YOUR TRUST, AT LEAST FOR A WHILE.

MOST DISAGREEMENTS ARE MIS-UNDERSTANDINGS THAT STEM FROM PRIVATE, UNRELATED PROBLEMS. BEFORE YOU REACT, TRY FIRST TO SEE THE MOTIVE BEHIND THE BEHAVIOR.

PETTY MATTERS CAN ASSUME GIGANTIC PROPORTIONS. SETTLE LITTLE ISSUES BEFORE THEY SIDETRACK YOUR VISION.

"A GENTLE ANSWER TURNS AWAY WRATH, BUT A HARSH WORD STIRS UP ANGER" (PROVERBS 15:1).

Genesis 50:15-21

When Joseph's brothers saw that their father was dead, they said, "What if Joseph holds a grudge against us and pays us back for all the wrongs we did to him?"

So they sent word to Joseph, saying, "Your father left these instructions before he died: 'This is what you are to say to Joseph: I ask you to forgive your brothers the sins and the wrongs they committed in treating you so badly.' Now please forgive the sins of the servants of the God of your father." When their message came to him, Joseph wept.

His brothers then came and threw themselves down before him. "We are your slaves," they said.

But Joseph said to them, "Don't be afraid. Am I in the place of God? You intended to harm me, but God intended it for good to accomplish what is now being done, the saving of many lives.

"So then, don't be afraid. I will provide for you and your children." And he reassured them and spoke kindly to them.

THE VOICE OF WISDOM

Leonardo da Vinci had a violent quarrel with a fellow painter shortly before he began work on The Last Supper. As he began to paint, his anger led him to paint the face of this man who was now his enemy into the face of Judas. This was da Vinci's revenge, and he was gleeful over what he had done.

He painted the other disciples and was pleased with his work. But when he started to paint the face of Christ, his best efforts failed. He could no longer see the Savior he longed to honor. Through his struggle, he realized that he must forgive his fellow painter and erase his face from that of Judas. Only then was da Vinci able to see Jesus clearly and paint His face onto the canvas.

Like da Vinci, we too have difficulty seeing Jesus clearly when the sin of unforgiveness comes between us and someone who has offended us. A colleague may have questioned a decision we made in a committee meeting. A friend may have hurt us by breaking a confidence. But Jesus calls us to forgive–again and again–those who cause our pain. "I tell you, not seven times, but seventy times seven."

–CHIP RICKS

It's terrible to have people you feel the need to avoid because of unresolved conflict. Talk about it. Get it out in the open.

LEADERSHIP COSTS

People see your name on the program, your picture in the paper.
If they could only see what goes on behind the scenes.

MOSES BEING PUNISHED? AFTER ONE LITTLE SLIP-UP? LEADERSHIP COMES WITH GRAVE RESPONSIBILITIES . . . AND THE WILLINGNESS TO SEE THIS AS BEING FAIR.

━━━ ◈ ━━━

BE CAREFUL OF WHAT YOU DEMAND AS YOUR RIGHTS. EXPECT TO WORK HARDER THAN ANYONE WHO ANSWERS TO YOU.

━━━ ◈ ━━━

WORK HARD TO MAKE SURE THAT YOUR FAMILY AND CHILDREN AREN'T THE ONES PAYING THE BIGGEST PRICE FOR YOUR OUTSIDE COMMITMENTS.

━━━ ◈ ━━━

OTHERS ARE WATCHING TO SEE HOW YOU HANDLE YOUR STRESSES. IS GOD PLEASED BY WHAT THEY SEE?

Numbers 20:2, 7-12

Now there was no water for the community, and the people gathered in opposition to Moses and Aaron. . . .

The LORD said to Moses, "Take the staff, and you and your brother Aaron gather the assembly together. Speak to that rock before their eyes and it will pour out its water. You will bring water out of the rock for the community so that they and their livestock can drink."

So Moses took the staff from the LORD's presence, just as he commanded him.

He and Aaron gathered the assembly together in front of the rock and Moses said to them, "Listen, you rebels, must we bring you water out of this rock?"

Then Moses raised his arm and struck the rock twice with his staff. Water gushed out, and the community and their livestock drank.

But the LORD said to Moses and Aaron, "Because you did not trust in me enough to honor me as holy in the sight of the Israelites, you will not bring this community into the land I give them."

THE VOICE OF WISDOM

Whenever I find myself feeling weary and overwhelmed by the commitments I've made to my family, friends, publishers, and the Women of Faith tour, I remember Jesus' words: "From everyone who has been given much, much will be demanded; and from the one who has been entrusted with much, much more will be asked" (Luke 12:48).

Many blessings have been given to me. I know God didn't bless me with these gifts so I could sit back in the recliner and keep them all to myself.

Sometimes life becomes so complicated that we feel as if we've gone as far as we can down this stressful highway. We imagine ourselves smashed up against a brick wall, unable to answer one more call, hear one more complaint, and take one more breath.

When that's the image that fills your mind, change the brick wall to God. Imagine yourself pressed tightly against his heart, wrapped in his everlasting arms, soothed by his life-giving support. Picture yourself encircled in God's love, soaked in His strength. Then step out onto the highway once more.

–BARBARA JOHNSON

Let the rest of the world sleep in on Saturdays and waste their talents on meaningless trivia. You have a job to do.

NO NEED TO THANK ME

You may have to go weeks and months between compliments,
but you can live off God's seal of approval any day.

THE WORD FOR THE DAY

WHETHER EVERYONE SEES OR NO ONE SEES, YOUR WORK HAS VALUE THAT GOD CAN SEE.

TOO MUCH IS MADE OF TITLES AND ACCOMPLISHMENTS. WE ARE VALUED "NOT BECAUSE OF ANYTHING WE HAVE DONE, BUT BECAUSE OF HIS OWN PURPOSE AND GRACE."

WHETHER AT WORK IN THE TRENCHES OR CONFINED IN PRISON, PAUL KNEW THAT GOD WAS THE ONE BRINGING ABOUT THE RESULTS.

YOU CAN'T DEPEND ON ENCOURAGEMENT, BUT YOU CAN'T LEAD WITHOUT GIVING IT.

2 Timothy 1:8-12, 14

So do not be ashamed to testify about our Lord, or ashamed of me his prisoner. But join with me in suffering for the gospel, by the power of God, who has saved us and called us to a holy life—not because of anything we have done but because of his own purpose and grace.

This grace was given us in Christ Jesus before the beginning of time, but it has now been revealed through the appearing of our Savior, Christ Jesus, who has destroyed death and has brought life and immortality to light through the gospel.

And of this gospel I was appointed a herald and an apostle and a teacher. That is why I am suffering as I am. Yet I am not ashamed, because I know whom I have believed, and am convinced that he is able to guard what I have entrusted to him for that day....

Guard the good deposit that was entrusted to you—guard it with the help of the Holy Spirit who lives in us.

THE VOICE OF WISDOM

As I have grown in faith and confidence, I have known more and more that my worth is based on the love of God. Nothing I can do will make me special. No awards I can earn will make me a better person. The taproot of my being grows in the rich soil of the being of Christ instead of in the shifting sands of worldly accomplishment.

The problem with developing a good resumé is that it is a bottomless pit. The ideal person we want to be remains just a few accomplishments short of our vitas. No matter how many poems we publish, how many job offers we receive, we really need more to prove to ourselves–and to others we consider "important" –that we are worthy of respect. Like the shimmering puddle in the middle of the highway, the mirage of self-contentment lies just down the road.

The great freedom Jesus gives us is to be ourselves, defined by His love and our inner qualities and gifts rather than by any kind of show we put on for the world. We are freed, like uncaged birds, because God loves us unconditionally–without degrees, promotions, elected offices, or a cool crowd surrounding us.

–LESLIE WILLIAMS

Leadership & Principle

NUMBER 78

LEADERS DON'T NEED CONSTANT APPROVAL TO VALIDATE THEIR WORK.

The correct posture of the Christian is neither haughtiness nor false humility, but a calm assurance of your role in God's plan.

WORK IN PROGRESS

The fruits of your labors will only taste as sweet as the grateful attitude you've used in completing your work.

THE WORD FOR THE DAY

NOAH HAD GOOD HELP AND THE APPROVAL OF GOD DURING HIS **100**-YEAR BOAT PROJECT, BUT EVEN THESE BLESSINGS DIDN'T NEGATE HIS NEED FOR HARD WORK.

"HE WHO WORKS HIS LAND WILL HAVE ABUNDANT FOOD, BUT HE WHO CHASES FANTASIES LACKS JUDGMENT" (PROVERBS 12:11).

CHECK REGULARLY TO BE SURE YOUR HARD WORK IS AS PRODUCTIVE AS IT IS DILIGENT.

"NOAH DID EVERYTHING JUST AS GOD COMMANDED HIM." THIS SHOULD BE THE HEARTBEAT OF EVERY CHRISTIAN LEADER.

Genesis 6:13-16, 19-22

So God said to Noah, "I am going to put an end to all people, for the earth is filled with violence because of them. I am surely going to destroy both them and the earth.

"So make yourself an ark of cypress wood; make rooms in it and coat it with pitch inside and out. This is how you are to build it: The ark is to be 450 feet long, 75 feet wide and 45 feet high.

"Make a roof for it and finish the ark to within 18 inches of the top. Put a door in the side of the ark and make lower, middle and upper decks...."

"You are to bring into the ark two of all living creatures, male and female, to keep them alive with you. Two of every kind of bird, of every kind of animal and of every kind of creature that moves along the ground will come to you to be kept alive. You are to take every kind of food that is to be eaten and store it away as food for you and for them."

Noah did everything just as God commanded him.

THE VOICE OF WISDOM

Is work a necessary evil, even a curse? A Christian who spent many years in Soviet work camps, learning to know work at its most brutal, its most degrading and dehumanizing, testified that he took pride in it, did the best he could, worked to the limit of his strength each day. Why? Because he saw it as a gift from God, coming to him from the hand of God, the very will of God for him. He remembered that Jesus did not make benches and roofbeams and plow handles by means of miracles, but by means of saw, axe, and adze.

Wouldn't it make an astounding difference, not only in the quality of the work we do, but also in the satisfaction, even our joy, if we recognized God's gracious gift in every single task? If our children saw us doing "heartily as unto the Lord" all the work we do, they would learn true happiness. Instead of feeling that they must be allowed to do what they like, they would learn to like what they do.

As we make an offering of our work, we find the truth of a principle Jesus taught: Fulfillment is not a goal to achieve, but always the by-product of sacrifice.

–ELISABETH ELLIOT

You can expect a reward from all your hard work–not by how much you've done, but by how well you've done it.

CHECK YOUR CALENDAR

Your day planner can quickly get to be a real handful.
But how'd you like to get a better grip on your time?

THE PROVERBS 31 WOMAN CAN EASILY BE A SOURCE OF GUILT AND FRUSTRATION—OR A CHALLENGE TO MAKE EVERY MINUTE COUNT.

⸺ ☙ ⸺

NOTICE HER INVOLVEMENT IN FAMILY, WORK, HOME, AND MINISTRY. STRIVE TO MAINTAIN A PROPER BALANCE.

⸺ ☙ ⸺

UP EARLY, TO BED LATE. SOUND FAMILIAR? A GOOD NIGHT'S SLEEP SHOULD NOT BE A CONSTANT CASUALTY OF YOUR BUSY SCHEDULE.

⸺ ☙ ⸺

BEING IDLE IS PROBABLY NOT YOUR PROBLEM. BUT CHOOSE ACTIVITIES CAREFULLY FOR THE IDLE TIME YOU DO HAVE.

Proverbs 31:13–22, 27

She selects wool and flax and works with eager hands.

She is like the merchant ships, bringing her food from afar.

She gets up while it is still dark; she provides food for her family and portions for her servant girls.

She considers a field and buys it; out of her earnings she plants a vineyard.

She sets about her work vigorously; her arms are strong for her tasks.

She sees that her trading is profitable, and her lamp does not go out at night.

In her hand she holds the distaff and grasps the spindle with her fingers.

She opens her arms to the poor and extends her hands to the needy.

When it snows, she has no fear for her household; for all of them are clothed in scarlet.

She makes coverings for her bed; she is clothed in fine linen and purple. . . .

She watches over the affairs of her household and does not eat the bread of idleness.

THE VOICE OF WISDOM

"I don't have time" is probably a lie more often than not, covering for "I don't want to." We have time—twenty-four hours a day, seven days a week. Demands on our time differ, of course, and it is here that the disciple must refer to his Master. There will be time for everything God wants us to do.

There were endless demands on Jesus' time. People pressed on Him with their needs so that He and His disciples had not leisure even to eat, and He would go away into the hills to pray and be alone.

Still, He was able to make that amazing claim, "I have finished the work you gave me to do" (John 17:4). This was not the same as saying He had finished everything He could possibly think of to do or that He had done everything others had asked. The claim was that He had done what had been given.

This is an important clue for us. The work of God is appointed. *There is always enough time to do the will of God.* When we find ourselves frantic and frustrated, harried and harassed, it is a sign that we are running on our own schedule, not on God's.

–ELISABETH ELLIOT

If you never feel like you're accomplishing enough, maybe it's because you're trying to do too much.

THE REAL WORLD

It would be nice if we didn't have to worry about the larger issues of our culture. But that wouldn't be leadership.

THE WORD FOR THE DAY

OUR KINGDOM IS NOT OF THIS WORLD, BUT WE HAVE A RESPONSIBILITY TO ITS PEOPLE, TO WORK FOR THEIR GOOD, TO FIGHT FOR THEIR SOULS.

UNDERSTANDING THE TIMES CAN HELP YOU KEEP YOUR VISION IN TUNE WITH THE REAL NEEDS AROUND YOU.

YOU'LL PROBABLY LEARN MORE FROM LISTENING TO PEOPLE THAN FROM READING MAGAZINES AND WATCHING THE HEADLINES.

WITH SO MUCH INFORMATION AVAILABLE, YOU MUST ASK GOD TO HELP DISCERN THE THINGS YOU TRULY NEED TO KNOW.

2 Timothy 3:1-5, 12-15

But mark this: There will be terrible times in the last days.

People will be lovers of themselves, lovers of money, boastful, proud, abusive, disobedient to their parents, ungrateful, unholy, without love, unforgiving, slanderous, without self-control, brutal, not lovers of the good, treacherous, rash, conceited, lovers of pleasure rather than lovers of God–having a form of godliness but denying its power. Have nothing to do with them. . . .

In fact, everyone who wants to live a godly life in Christ Jesus will be persecuted, while evil men and impostors will go from bad to worse, deceiving and being deceived.

But as for you, continue in what you have learned and have become convinced of, because you know those from whom you learned it, and how from infancy you have known the holy Scriptures, which are able to make you wise for salvation through faith in Christ Jesus.

THE VOICE OF WISDOM

Twenty years from now, my grandchildren are going to look at me and ask, "Me-mommie, what were you doing when America was going through a cultural war and biblical truth was being distorted?" I am not about to say, "Oh, I shopped till I dropped!" or "Well, I improved my golf game," or "That was dirty work, and I couldn't get involved because I may have broken my acrylic fingernails."

Of course, there is nothing wrong with shopping, golf, or even acrylic fingernails, but sometimes it seems as if many women have slipped into a comfortable cocoon, and they never emerge. If you talk about the reality of abortion, pornography, abuse, or AIDS, they look at you with their eyes glossed over as if you are talking about something in outer space. They act as if there is no world beyond their cocoon. And yet that is the world their grandchildren are growing up in. I am terrified of that cocoon. I plead with the Lord to never let me slip into such creature comfort that I am no longer an aroma of the knowledge of Christ to a hurting world.

–SUSAN HUNT

Leadership & Principle

NUMBER 81

GOOD LEADERS POSSESS A BROAD UNDERSTANDING OF THE TIMES IN WHICH THEY LIVE.

The newscasts are cutting edge, but the Bible continues to speak to this age. Ask God to let it speak to you clearly.

SEEING THE CHANGE

*Imagine a world where everything always stays the same,
because that's the only place where a world like that exists.*

THE WORD FOR THE DAY

CHANGE CAN BE AS SCARY AS
A MURDEROUS SAUL MUST
HAVE SEEMED TO THE EARLY
CHURCH. BUT GOOD THINGS
CAN COME AS A RESULT OF IT.

⸎

IMPROVE YOUR OWN LEADER-
SHIP ABILITY BY STRIVING TO
STAY ONE STEP AHEAD OF THE
CHANGE CYCLES.

⸎

BUT EVEN IN TIMES OF
CHANGE, YOU SHOULD POSSESS
SOME THINGS THAT *NEVER*
CHANGE—VALUES YOU'D
DEFEND NO MATTER WHAT.

⸎

THE BEST LEADERSHIP STYLES
MIX THE OLD WITH THE NEW,
STAYING CURRENT WITHOUT
BECOMING RUDDERLESS.

Acts 9:19b-22, 26-28

Saul spent several days with the disciples in Damascus. At once he began to preach in the synagogues that Jesus is the Son of God.

All those who heard him were astonished and asked, "Isn't he the man who caused havoc in Jerusalem among those who call on this name? And hasn't he come here to take them as prisoners to the chief priests?"

Yet Saul grew more and more powerful and baffled the Jews living in Damascus by proving that Jesus is the Christ. . . .

When he came to Jerusalem, he tried to join the disciples, but they were all afraid of him, not believing that he really was a disciple.

But Barnabas took him and brought him to the apostles. He told them how Saul on his journey had seen the Lord and that the Lord had spoken to him, and how in Damascus he had preached fearlessly in the name of Jesus.

So Saul stayed with them and moved about freely in Jerusalem, speaking boldly in the name of the Lord.

THE VOICE OF WISDOM

Henry Ford was born on a Michigan farm during the Civil War. His childhood was spent tinkering with threshers, reapers, and other horse-drawn farm equipment. When he was twelve, Ford saw a steam-driven traction engine. From then on, engines were his passion. He was ready to let go of the past.

When he was sixteen, Ford went to Detroit as an apprentice machinist. Eventually, he became chief engineer for the Edison Illuminating Company. Ford, however, was intrigued by a recent invention, an internal combustion engine powered by gasoline. His wife shared his enthusiasm, and his earliest models were tested on their kitchen table.

All of America was automobile mad, Ford along with them. When he was an apprentice machinist, he had an idea for mass producing inexpensive pocket watches. He adapted this concept, and it became the basis for the automobile assembly line.

Soon an automobile was within reach of nearly every American family. He had developed a manufacturing system that gave us freedom of movement, and changed the world.

–SHEILA MURRAY BETHEL

Leadership & Principle

NUMBER 82

A NEW DAY OFTEN CALLS FOR A NEW STRATEGY, A NEW SHAPE, A WHOLE NEW APPROACH.

When changes have upset your world, try to remember that God has seen it all before. And lived to tell about it.

LIFELONG LEARNING

Leaders love to teach, to motivate, to inform.
But it all goes back to a love even deeper than these—a love of learning.

THE WORD FOR THE DAY

LEARNING IS WHAT LEADERS DO WHILE THE REST OF THE WORLD IS WATCHING TV AND READING CEREAL BOXES.

———— ❧ ————

THERE'S A LOT OF SO-CALLED WISDOM OUT THERE THAT EVEN TALKS ABOUT A SO-CALLED GOD. BE SURE YOUR ADOPTED TRUTHS COME FROM THE ONE TRUE AUTHOR.

———— ❧ ————

YOU CAN'T LIVE ON BORROWED KNOWLEDGE. READING AND FIRSTHAND OBSERVATION WILL MAKE WISDOM YOURS.

———— ❧ ————

"WISDOM IS SUPREME; THERE-FORE GET WISDOM. THOUGH IT COST ALL YOU HAVE, GET UNDERSTANDING"
(PROVERBS 4:7).

1 Kings 10:1-3, 6-8

When the queen of Sheba heard about the fame of Solomon and his relation to the name of the LORD, she came to test him with hard questions.

Arriving at Jerusalem with a very great cara-van—with camels carrying spices, large quantities of gold, and precious stones—she came to Solomon and talked with him about all that she had on her mind.

Solomon answered all her questions; nothing was too hard for the king to explain to her. . . .

She said to the king, "The report I heard in my own country about your achievements and your wisdom is true.

But I did not believe these things until I came and saw with my own eyes. Indeed, not even half was told me; in wisdom and wealth you have far exceeded the report I heard.

How happy your men must be! How happy your officials, who continually stand before you and hear your wisdom!"

THE VOICE OF WISDOM

Slowly, the long caravan crept along the ascending road from Jericho to Jerusalem. It had taken weeks to cover more than two thousand miles. The cold nights and scorchingly hot days had seemed endless. The countryside had been as sunbaked and unpleasant as a moonscape. Worst of all were the lashing sandstorms and raging winds of the wilderness. But in her heart, she knew she must go. At home in her royal palace in Sheba, she had heard repeatedly about Solomon, the king of Israel, the man who appeared to be immensely rich and unbelievably wise. The whole earth consulted Solomon to hear the wisdom God had put in his heart. And she had many questions–about her personal life, about her royal obligations, about God.

The way the queen ordered her priorities proves she was a wise woman. In her wisdom, she accepted the limitations of her own knowledge and insight. She wanted to know more and was willing to make many sacrifices in order to gain wisdom. Her time, money, and effort were spent in attaining this goal.

–GIEN KARSSEN

Leadership Principle

NUMBER 83

LEADERS NEVER STOP LEARNING.

The desire is already there. The challenge is clearing some spots in your week where learning can become a habit.

PEOPLE MATTER MOST

We all deal with certain people who can get under our skin. But no one in our lives should be beneath our dignity.

THE WORD FOR THE DAY

ADD TO YOUR LIST OF TALENTS AND ACCOMPLISHMENTS THE ABILITY TO BE BIGGER THAN OTHERS' DIFFERENCES.

❧

"NO ONE HAS EVER SEEN GOD, BUT IF WE LOVE ONE ANOTHER, GOD LIVES IN US AND HIS LOVE IS MADE COMPLETE IN US"
(1 JOHN 4:12).

❧

YOU DON'T HAVE TO LIKE SOMEONE TO WANT THE BEST FOR THEM, AND TO WORK FOR THEIR GOOD EVEN WHEN THEY'VE BEEN A PROBLEM.

❧

THE TIME MAY COME FOR YOU TO DISMISS SOMEONE FROM YOUR WORK FORCE, BUT NEVER FROM YOUR PRAYER LIST.

1 Corinthians 12:31b–13:8a, 13

And now I will show you the most excellent way.

If I speak in the tongues of men and of angels, but have not love, I am only a resounding gong or a clanging cymbal.

If I have the gift of prophecy and can fathom all mysteries and all knowledge, and if I have a faith that can move mountains, but have not love, I am nothing.

If I give all I possess to the poor and surrender my body to the flames, but have not love, I gain nothing.

Love is patient, love is kind. It does not envy, it does not boast, it is not proud.

It is not rude, it is not self-seeking, it is not easily angered, it keeps no record of wrongs.

Love does not delight in evil but rejoices with the truth. It always protects, always trusts, always hopes, always perseveres.

Love never fails. . . .

And now these three remain: faith, hope and love. But the greatest of these is love.

THE VOICE OF WISDOM

I walked into a Dallas bank to meet with an executive vice president about customer service training. I went up to the secretary's desk, smiled, and announced my name and my reason for being there. The secretary stopped working, looked me up and down, gave me no response, stood up, and walked off, leaving me standing there. She had decided I wasn't worth a nod, let alone a smile or a handshake.

When I taught the customer service class, she was a top participant. She was pleasant, positive, polite, and poised. But none of that held any meaning for me. Her lasting impression remained my first impression of her.

But I wasn't following Christ's admonition to give people room to make a second impression. I needed to give her a second chance.

Maybe you've written a person off as someone you want nothing to do with. That person just might deserve a second chance.

God knows us inside out and outside in. He understands what motivates us and accepts us even in our worst moments. I want to be able to do the same for others.

–THELMA WELLS

Leadership Principle

NUMBER 84

PEOPLE ARE NOT EXPENDABLE.

Get that certain person's face up close in your mind today. And ask God for the grace to love the way He loves.

PASSING THE TORCH

*Responsible leadership requires that you leave your position
of power in even better hands than you received it.*

THE WORD FOR THE DAY

NO MATTER HOW LONG IT LASTS, OUR TIME OF LEADER-SHIP IS SHORT—TOO SHORT TO IGNORE THE NEED FOR TRAIN-ING NEW LEADERS FOR TOMORROW.

———— ✒ ————

CAN YOU NAME ONE EMERGING LEADER YOU WOULD COMMIT TO INVESTING YOURSELF IN?

———— ✒ ————

IN TALKING TO HIS DISCIPLES, JESUS DIDN'T CANDY-COAT THE TASTE OF RESPONSIBILITY. HE PAINTED THE PICTURE IN REAL-LIFE COLORS.

———— ✒ ————

JESUS ALSO ASKED HIS FOL-LOWERS TO REPORT BACK TO HIM. BUILD INTO YOUR FOL-LOWERS THE ACCOUNTABILITY OF YOUR OWN EVALUATION.

Luke 10:1-2, 16, 22-24

After this the Lord appointed seventy-two others and sent them two by two ahead of him to every town and place where he was about to go.

He told them, "The harvest is plentiful, but the workers are few. Ask the Lord of the harvest, therefore, to send out workers into his harvest field. . . .

"He who listens to you listens to me; he who rejects you rejects me; but he who rejects me rejects him who sent me. . . .

"All things have been committed to me by my Father. No one knows who the Son is except the Father, and no one knows who the Father is except the Son and those to whom the Son chooses to reveal him."

Then he turned to his disciples and said privately, "Blessed are the eyes that see what you see.

"For I tell you that many prophets and kings wanted to see what you see but did not see it, and to hear what you hear but did not hear it."

THE VOICE OF WISDOM

I personally witnessed the downfall of an executive director who had ruled a huge organization for nearly twelve years, largely through smoke and mirrors. When his incompetence finally came collapsing down upon him and he was relieved of his command, there was quite a mess to clean up. The problem was, it wasn't just his incompetence that had to be corrected. He had multiplied himself by hiring people who were far less qualified, and hence less of a threat to him in every area. This organization had a core of incompetence that, like a cancer, had infiltrated every department and nearly caused the demise of the entire organization.

By contrast, Jesus as a CEO was eager and intent upon hiring people he felt could replace him. "Greater things than I have done shall you do," he promised. Jesus did not hoard or guard the power of his office. He kept teaching and sharing and demonstrating it so team members would learn that they, too, had the power to do what he had done. Jesus trained his replacements.

–LAURIE BETH JONES

Leadership Principle

NUMBER 85

QUALITY LEADERS PREPARE FOR THE FUTURE BY TRAINING THEIR SUCCESSORS.

Stay constantly on the lookout for those in your organization who are showing signs of something greater.

I'M COUNTING ON ME

Some things in your job description don't fall into your list of talents and strengths. But they do fall to you to do them.

WHAT DO YOU DO WHEN YOU FEEL OUTMATCHED, OVER-STRESSED, AND UNDERQUALI-FIED? THE BEST YOU CAN.

⟨≈⟩

GOD HAS WAYS TO REMIND HIGH ACHIEVERS WHO THE SOURCE OF THEIR STRENGTH IS.

⟨≈⟩

PAUL ACCOMPLISHED A LOT IN HIS MINISTRY—MUCH OF WHICH CAME NATURALLY TO HIS TALENTS AND TEMPERA-MENT. BUT HIS GREATEST SUC-CESSES WERE THOSE THAT CAME THE HARDEST.

⟨≈⟩

ARE YOU ABLE YET TO "DELIGHT" IN THE PARTS OF YOUR WORK THAT REQUIRE YOU TO STRETCH, TO DIG, TO GROW?

2 Corinthians 11:27-29a, 30, 12:7-10

I have labored and toiled and have often gone without sleep; I have known hunger and thirst and have often gone without food; I have been cold and naked. Besides everything else, I face daily the pressure of my concern for all the churches.

Who is weak, and I do not feel weak? . . . If I must boast, I will boast of the things that show my weakness. . . .

To keep me from becoming conceited because of these surpassingly great revelations, there was given me a thorn in my flesh, a messenger of Satan, to torment me. Three times I pleaded with the Lord to take it away from me.

But he said to me, "My grace is sufficient for you, for my power is made perfect in weakness." Therefore I will boast all the more gladly about my weaknesses, so that Christ's power may rest on me.

That is why, for Christ's sake, I delight in weaknesses, in insults, in hardships, in persecutions, in difficulties. For when I am weak, then I am strong.

Thank you, Lord, that there are so many people I can depend on for so many things. But there is another person I must learn to depend on even more, Lord: myself.

You gave each of us areas of life where we can't lean on anybody else. No other person can keep my promises to others or to me. For that, all that, I've got to depend on myself.

Help me to remember this. God, give me belief in myself and the will power to act on that belief. Thank you for gradually guiding me into habits that fortify that faith, so that at the end of each day I can realize, "I didn't let me down. I did what I promised myself."

And even when I undertake too much, when I set my sights too high, when I project goals a little beyond my reach, help me not to get discouraged. Rather, help me realize that delay doesn't mean defeat. Despite a hundred detours, I will keep driving in the right direction.

I will not quit. I will keep my commitments. Make me always able to depend on myself.

—MARJORIE HOLMES

Leadership Principle

NUMBER 86

LEADERS RECOGNIZE THEIR WEAKNESSES, BUT WORK HARD TO OVERCOME THEM.

The parts of your day which you look forward to the least may be the very ones where you grow the most character.

WHAT ABOUT NOW?

Later is a convenient place to park the tasks of leadership.
But there may already be too many cars waiting out there.

NOT EVERYTHING THAT CROSSES YOUR DESK IS A PRIORITY ITEM. BUT EVERYTHING MUST BE CHECKED TO SEE IF IT IS.

───── ◈ ─────

JAMES CALLED IT "BOASTING" WHEN WE ASSUME THAT TOMORROW WILL BE JUST LIKE TODAY. "WHY, YOU DO NOT EVEN KNOW WHAT WILL HAPPEN TOMORROW." BETTER TO GET AS MUCH DONE TODAY AS WE CAN, AND LEAVE TOMORROW TO THE LORD.

───── ◈ ─────

THE WISEST THING TO DO WITH MANY OF THE TASKS YOU FACE MAY INDEED BE TO DELAY THEM. THAT'S NOT PROCRASTINATING. THAT'S BRING PROACTIVE.

James 4:13–17
Proverbs 3:25–28

Now listen, you who say, "Today or tomorrow we will go to this or that city, spend a year there, carry on business and make money."

Why, you do not even know what will happen tomorrow. What is your life? You are a mist that appears for a little while and then vanishes.

Instead, you ought to say, "If it is the Lord's will, we will live and do this or that."

As it is, you boast and brag. All such boasting is evil. Anyone, then, who knows the good he ought to do and doesn't do it, sins. . . .

Have no fear of sudden disaster or of the ruin that overtakes the wicked, for the LORD will be your confidence and will keep your foot from being snared.

Do not withhold good from those who deserve it, when it is in your power to act. Do not say to your neighbor, "Come back later; I'll give it tomorrow" –when you now have it with you.

THE VOICE OF WISDOM

What is the best use of my time, right now? Ask yourself this question all through the day, particularly if you are not positive about whether you are using your time to your best advantage. Ask it when you complete a task or are at a natural transition, when you've been interrupted by a visitor or a phone call, or when you are torn between two different projects.

If you struggle with procrastination, you are not alone. How often have we echoed the Apostle Paul's apparent self-reproach as he wrote to the Romans, "I do not understand what I do. For what I want to do, I do not do" (Romans 7:15). We cannot easily transform the bad habits of procrastination that took years to acquire. But by thoughtful analysis of the reasons for our postponing, we can alter our attitude toward the problem. And changed attitudes become a springboard for modified behavior.

We procrastinators with good intentions would do well to adhere to the challenge of the Apostle Paul in another letter: "On with it, then, and finish the job! Be as eager to finish it as you were to plan it" (2 Cor. 8:11).
–DEBBIE LLOYD

Leadership & Principle

NUMBER 87

PROCRASTINATION WILL CATCH UP WITH YOU WHEN YOU LEAST EXPECT IT.

Before you put one more thing off until tomorrow, give the option of doing it today a fair and firm consideration.

HEALTH WISE

The life of a leader calls for eat-out lunches and work-over weekends.
That's why it also calls for healthy disciplines.

THE WORD FOR THE DAY

LIFE SETS BEFORE YOU A TRAY OF UNHEALTHY EXPECTATIONS. THAT DOESN'T MEAN YOU HAVE TO BITE.

———— ❦ ————

THE KING'S REGIMEN WENT AGAINST DANIEL'S CONSCIENCE. BUT HE VERY GRACIOUSLY, VERY REASONABLY OBJECTED. YOU DON'T HAVE TO BE PUSHY TO PUSH AWAY FROM THE WORLD'S TABLE.

———— ❦ ————

HEALTHY HABITS CAN CUT INTO YOUR SCHEDULE, BUT ADD YEARS TO YOUR EFFECTIVENESS.

———— ❦ ————

"YOU ARE NOT YOUR OWN; YOU WERE BOUGHT AT A PRICE. THEREFORE HONOR GOD WITH YOUR BODY"

(1 CORINTHIANS 6:19-20)

Daniel 1:8-10, 12-15

But Daniel resolved not to defile himself with the royal food and wine, and he asked the chief official for permission not to defile himself in this way.

Now God had caused the official to show favor and sympathy to Daniel, but the official told Daniel, "I am afraid of my lord the king, who has assigned your food and drink. Why should he see you looking worse than the other young men of your age? The king would then have my head because of you...."

"Please test your servants for ten days: Give us nothing but vegetables to eat and water to drink. Then compare our appearance with that of the young men who eat the royal food, and treat your servants in accordance with what you see."

So he agreed to this and tested them for ten days.

At the end of the ten days they looked healthier and better nourished than any of the young men who ate the royal food.

THE VOICE OF WISDOM

We live in a high-stress society. Almost every time we turn around, someone asks us to do something else. Our responsibilities pile high at the office, at home, and at church. A proper motivation for healthy living and weight loss is to better manage the stress in your life. It's clear to me that as we get our weight, nutrition, and exercise under control, our stress level becomes more tolerable. Although I have a stressful job, with twenty-five employees and a heavy travel schedule, I do not suffer from stress. I believe there are four reasons for this:

1. I have a daily quiet time with God each morning where I give the day to Him. He is in charge of my time and schedule.

2. I exercise five days a week. While running, I solve problems and plan my day.

3. I am not a worrier. As a child I learned from my mother that the things we worry about never happen. I believe worry is a great stress producer.

4. I get plenty of rest and take time off to play. Rest and leisure time are prerequisites to a stress-free life.

–CAROLE LEWIS

Leadership & Principle

NUMBER 88

COMMIT YOURSELF TO A HEALTHY LIFESTYLE.

The Bible says that your body is a temple of the Holy Spirit. You're living in God's house. Don't junk it up.

STEADY AS SHE GOES

You bring so much of yourself into your leadership role.
But unchecked emotions can bring your leadership down.

THE WORD FOR THE DAY

TRY TO VIEW YOUR PERSONAL DISPUTES AND DIFFERENCES IN AN ETERNAL LIGHT. WHEN YOU LOSE YOUR TEMPER, IT USUALLY MEANS YOU'VE LOST YOUR PERSPECTIVE.

YOUR LEADERSHIP AND AUTHORITY ARE BUILT ON TRUST. OTHERS MUST BE ABLE TO COUNT ON YOU KEEPING YOUR COOL IN TENSE SITUATIONS.

CONTROLLING YOUR EMOTIONS ALSO MEANS USING THEIR ENERGY TO MOTIVATE AND EXCEL.

DON'T TAKE WHAT PEOPLE SAY ABOUT YOU OR YOUR WORK TOO PERSONALLY. LET GOD BE THE JUDGE OF THAT.

1 Peter 4:7-11, 13-14

The end of all things is near. Therefore be clear minded and self-controlled so that you can pray.

Above all, love each other deeply, because love covers over a multitude of sins. Offer hospitality to one another without grumbling.

Each one should use whatever gift he has received to serve others, faithfully administering God's grace in its various forms.

If anyone speaks, he should do it as one speaking the very words of God. If anyone serves, he should do it with the strength God provides, so that in all things God may be praised through Jesus Christ. To him be the glory and the power for ever and ever. Amen. . . .

But rejoice that you participate in the sufferings of Christ, so that you may be overjoyed when his glory is revealed.

If you are insulted because of the name of Christ, you are blessed, for the Spirit of glory and of God rests on you.

THE VOICE OF WISDOM

In our efforts to develop emotional maturity, we must be careful to avoid both extremes: highs and lows.

Most of us have heard a great deal of teaching about emotional lows such as discouragement, depression, despondency, and despair. But we also need to avoid the other extreme, which is emotional highs.

God has shown me that if we give in to extreme highs, we are as out of balance as we are when we give in to extreme lows. To maintain an emotional balance, we need to stay on a level plain, somewhere between both extremes.

It may be hard for some people to maintain emotional stability because they are addicted to excitement. For some reason, they just can't seem to settle down and live ordinary, everyday lives like everyone else. Such people have to have something exciting going on all the time. If they don't, they soon get bored. Their search for excitement often leads to excessive emotional stimulation, not to the steady, deep-seated joy that is supposed to characterize the life of the believer. It is not wrong to be excited, but it is dangerous to be excessive.

–JOYCE MEYER

Leadership Principle

NUMBER 89

LEADERS MUST BE THE MASTERS OF THEIR EMOTIONS.

Get some Bible verses memorized and ready to use against the red flashes of anger and the dead weights of self-doubt.

IN HIS PRESENCE

The safest place in the world to lead is right in the presence of Almighty God. And you are there this very minute.

THE WORD FOR THE DAY

REMEMBER THAT EVEN THE ASPECTS OF YOUR LEADERSHIP WHICH TAKE PLACE BEHIND CLOSED DOORS ARE IN FULL VIEW OF THE EYES OF GOD.

PRAYER IS THE CONSTANT COMPANION OF THE CHRISTIAN LEADER.

LIVE AND LEAD IN SUCH A WAY THAT GOD'S PRESENCE IS SEEN AS A PRIVILEGE AND PROTECTION INSTEAD OF A PEST.

DO THE BEST YOU CAN. BUT TRUST GOD TO DO WHAT YOU CANNOT.

GOD IS YOUR GUIDE THROUGH THE CLOUDS OF CONFUSION, "FOR DARKNESS IS AS LIGHT" TO HIM.

Psalm 139:1-12

O LORD, you have searched me and you know me. You know when I sit and when I rise; you perceive my thoughts from afar.

You discern my going out and my lying down; you are familiar with all my ways. Before a word is on my tongue you know it completely, O LORD.

You hem me in–behind and before; you have laid your hand upon me. Such knowledge is too wonderful for me, too lofty for me to attain.

Where can I go from your Spirit? Where can I flee from your presence? If I go up to the heavens, you are there; if I make my bed in the depths, you are there.

If I rise on the wings of the dawn, if I settle on the far side of the sea, even there your hand will guide me, your right hand will hold me fast.

If I say, "Surely the darkness will hide me and the light become night around me," even the darkness will not be dark to you; the night will shine like the day, for darkness is as light to you.

THE VOICE OF WISDOM

This refreshing concept was introduced to me by Brother Lawrence, a lame monk working in a monastery kitchen. He said, "For me the time of action does not differ from the time of prayer, and in the noise and clatter of my kitchen, while several persons are calling on me for many different things, I possess God in as great tranquillity as when upon my knees."

As I read these words, I felt that our brother had probably become ensnared at one time or another in the trap of compartmentalization (time for work, time for prayer) and had realized this was not the way the Christian life was supposed to be. In desperation, he learned the secret of integration (incorporating the sacred with the secular), thereby sanctifying everything he did.

"Pray continually," the Bible commands (1 Thess. 5:17). Surely it is not suggesting a constantly repeated litany of petitions, which we are apt to call our prayers. Rather, it refers to prayer without an "s," which is more of a mind-set, a receptive approach to life around us, a consuming consciousness that God is.

–PEG RANKIN

Leadership Principle

NUMBER 90

EFFECTIVE LEADERS SEE THE INVISIBLE HAND OF GOD IN EVERY CIRCUMSTANCE OF LIFE.

Call out to God for help and direction in your quiet times, but always remember–He is there to help you all the time.

Scripture References Used

Scripture References Used

CREDITS

NOTES

NOTES

NOTES

NOTES

NOTES

NOTES